DRUGS

ADDICTION

&

INITIATION

DRUGS

ADDICTION

&

INITIATION

The Modern Search for Ritual

Luigi Zoja

Translated by
Marc E. Romano
and
Robert Mercurio

SIGO PRESS
Boston

Sigo Press
25 New Chardon Street, #8748, Boston, MA 02114

Publisher and Chief editor: Sisa Sternback
Associate Editor and translator: Marc E. Romano

Library of Congress Cataloging-in-Publication Data

Zoja, Luigi.
    Drugs, addiction, and initiation.

    Translation of: Nascere non basta.
    1. Drug abuse—Social aspects.   2. Drug abuse—
Psychological aspects.   3. Initiation rites.
I. Romano, Marc E.   II. Title.   [DNLM: 1. Substance
Abuse—psychology.   2. Ceremonial.   WM 270 Z85n]
HV5801.Z6513   1989   362.2'93   88-15851
ISBN 0-9384 34-39-X (pbk.)
ISBN 0-9384 34-38-1 (hardcover)

Cover: Coy Design
Printed in the USA

CONTENTS

To Stefano and Sara

FOREWORD

Attitudes towards drug addiction are continually changing, so much so that one might speak of them in terms of stylish currents. Fifteen years ago drug taking practically became a cult. Prophets like Timothy Leary spoke of "expanding consciousness," and numerous young people from all classes followed the drug apostles, these Pied Pipers from Hamelin. I recall an interview with a young drug-using couple. When the possible harmful effects of drug use were discussed, this turned out to be something completely incomprehensible to them. Only good can result from good. A drug high is something so marvellous that it would be against the law of nature if such a marvellous thing should have a pernicious effect in the long run.

Intellectuals in particular, who from the beginning enthusiastically took part in the drug cult, slowly became aware of the tragic results of drug abuse. But people did not quickly abandon what I would almost call the "worship of drug addicts." There arose everywhere a certain faithfulness towards drug addicts; people saw in them the helpless sacrifice of an angry society, sensitive people suffering for

us, who in our insensitivity hardly register the pervasive sickness of
our society.

Today the interest in drug addiction, the cult—and also the veneration of drug addicts as the sacrifice of an angry society—has subsided.
What remains are thousands of young people who are not getting off
drugs, and who end up as pitiable figures in public squares, producing
feelings of guilt, pity and dismay in passers-by.

Psychiatrists, psychologists, social workers, and not least the police,
wring their hands in daily despair about these apparently burnt-out
young people. A young man, numbed by drugs, passive, with only
one interest, to get the stuff again as soon as possible, is a profoundly
depressing sight. Where is the consciousness expanding effect then?
Is this really the conscious sacrifice of a brutal society?

Luigi Zoja helps us understand the phenomenon in all its contradictions. He brings drug addiction into its larger cultural context, but on
the other hand he does not use too high a style and does not lapse
into sentimentality.

He attempts to understand the drug problem in connection with
initiation, specifically with the absence of initiation rituals. On one
hand, rituals of initiation are something decidedly important; on the
other, the rituals that would satisfy these psychological needs today
are for the most part lost to us. There are at any rate still traces of these
initiation rituals all around us. I am reminded of the confirmation
celebrations of the Catholic and Protestant churches; and, in many
countries, military service is still experienced as an initiation. But all
of these are still vestiges; very many young people experience nothing
that even distantly approaches an introduction, an initiation into a
larger association with its secular and religious ideas.

Luigi Zoja did not write his book in order to stress the importance
of initiatory rituals. Most important to him is an understanding of drug
addicts, but in a subtle way he shows how the drug addict in his
addiction seeks initiation.

I find the present book to be of the greatest importance for anyone
who has anything to do with drug addicts. The danger is always that,
if one is involved with broken down, dispirited drug addicts, one
becomes discouraged, indeed even starts to despise them and forget
that a very complex and psychological process is playing itself out in

them. The cultural exaltation and veneration of drug users fifteen years ago was, after all, not completely groundless, at least not any more so than today's critical and accusatory stance towards them. Drug victims, either addicts or users, are not above all helpess weaklings, but rather fellow people who suffer under an unsatisfactory culural formation and often collapse upon it. The difficulties of understanding drug addicts are to keep all this constantly in view and to realize completely, on the one hand, the misery and the helplessness of these addicts and, on the other hand, the laudable attempt of these unhappy people to arrive, in a bizarre and almost perverse manner, at an initiation, at an introduction into the secrets of life.

Zoja is, like no one else, capable of understanding drug addiction. He has worked intensively in therapy with drug addicts, and thus has practical experience, but he is also a depth psychologist with a Jungian background, and as such he is in the position to recognize and take seriously the deeper motivations and the unfulfilled needs of drug addicts.

Strangely enough, one generally understands by "drugs" only a specific type of intoxicant, though not alcohol. But alcohol also a drug, and an alcoholic is a drug addict. Luigi Zoja is concerned in his book with drug addiction in the widest sense, including alcoholism. Every substance which causes mental alterations can be viewed as a drug and can make one addicted, be it a hard or a soft drug, be it hashish, LSD or heroin, be it alcohol or psychoactive substances.

There exists today the great danger that drug addiction—here taken in the widest sense—is understood only on the basis of individual psychopathology, and ultimately on the basis of a pathogenetic family history. In contrast to the attitude of fifteen years ago, the pendulum has swung all too much back to the other side. The larger cultural connections still interest only a few psychiatrists and psychologists. Zoja concerns himself with the problem of addiction not from a momentary stylish attitude; rather, he possesses a broader and temporally less specific overview of the phenomenon. His book is the expression of a deep care for a large group of suffering fellow people who need our understanding and our help.

Adolf Guggenbühl-Craig

CHAPTER 1

INTRODUCTION

The incest taboo is generally considered the most primordial, the most deeply rooted and widespread of cultural institutions. It is hard to imagine how vast and complex the consequences would be if that taboo were somehow to disappear. The same holds true for other cultural institutions, most strikingly that of initiation. In the introduction to his *Rites and Symbols of Initiation*, Mircea Eliade writes that the disappearance of initiation is in fact one of the principal differences between the ancient world and the modern.[1]

The institution of initiation was once almost as widespread and pervasive as the incest taboo, but its gradual dissolution is a relatively diffuse and more recent phenomenon, brought about for the first time by our own modern Western civilization. Not only do we lack any conclusions as far as the consequences of this loss are concerned, but the problem itself has only been addressed superficially, if at all. The only author who frequently addresses the problem is, once again, Eliade.

1. Eliade, M. *Rites and Symbols of Initiation.* New York: Harper & Row, 1958.

1

Initiation played a prominent role in all traditional societies not yet profaned by industrialization and modernization. In our contemporary culture, however, and especially in the last few decades, one seems to be able to identify various attempts at reviving initiation and the esoterism associated with it. In a society which tends toward the leveling out of "differences" in the negative sense of the word, the need to feel different in a positive sense is reawakening—the need to belong to an elect group possessing some additional and deeper truth.

We appear to live under conditions that are, for the most part, de-sacralized. However, it is enough just to scratch the surface of the situation to rediscover many elements of a real religious state, the survival of which manifests itself indirectly, especially in a need for esoteric and initiatory experiences. This study of initiation in its modern manifestations, though primarily based on depth psychology, will nonetheless refer directly to other disciplines, both because the various notes upon which this study is based already have a composite structure of their own (they are drawn from my seminars at the Milan Institute of the Italian Center of Analytical Psychology, subsequently amplified and presented in German at the C.G. Jung Institute, Zürich), and in order to avoid any psychological reductionism. The one area we have least called into play, and to which we have made only indirect references, is that of religion. This is certainly not due to lack of interest, since after all this entire study is dedicated to our sense of nostalgia for the sacred, but because I feel that religion is more a question of personal attitudes and convictions than it is a foundation upon which interpretations can be made.

Our approach has certain consequences on the interpretive models we will use. The fundamental structure of initiation stresses a "passage," but this can be seen as a passage from the profane to the sacred, or simultaneously as a passage through various phases of death and rebirth. The decision not to encroach directly upon the religious question dictates that we rely primarily on the second of the two initiatory models.

In the survival of the need for initiation, we will recognize above all a persistent desire for personal regeneration. We no longer have to speak of a latent need, since that need is today quite open and manifest. There exists a real demand for esoteric, initiatory experiences, yet those who cater to that demand are often unconscious of what they are doing. Even among those who profess themselves to be "masters" able to provide initiatory experiences we find a certain lack of awareness. Depth psychology itself often falls into the same trap, with offshoot groups straying into fields that are extraneous but tinted with esoterism. This is not to say that these "masters" are motivated by purely utilitarian concerns, but it should not be forgotten that becoming a "master" is often a self-serving compensation for personal problems.

In general, groups rather than individuals tend to assume initiatory functions, since not many individuals have the necessary experience to become masters. Such groups—cults ideological, religious, etc. . . .—tend to institutionalize the initiatory process, the various groups splintering into specialized sub-groups, a process of bureaucratization developing, all of which ensures the survival of the groups themselves, if not the satisfaction of their adherents' psychic needs. Unfortunately, the "rites" involved are often inventions of the intellect rather than attempts at consolidating truly meaningful experiences. Rites in any case are not invented, but arise over time and with the participation of many individuals, indeed of many generations.

The person who seeks instruction, the potential "adept," may be an individual with a complex personality who is unsatisfied by the traditional rules and truths of society. More often than not, he is a lonely person in search of fellowship, and his search is not for ordinary persons, but for "masters." His needs will only be partially satisfied, since what he will encounter above all are institutions which cannot respond to his deeper individual needs.

These institutions are generally able to provide information and even a genuine type of instruction, but not initiation. Mircea Eliade asserts that the only form of genuine initiatory structures today is in artistic-literary creation. All things considered, modern society is practically unable to provide institutional initiation. Such initiation calls for masters and structures formed over a long period of time and in context of a whole participating culture. Initiation presupposes that biological birth brings man into the world only partially, in an absolutely vegetative condition lacking values and transcendence.

Access to a higher state of being is possible only through symbolic and ritual death and regeneration.[2]

The first thing we should note is that, in order to produce rites and ceremonies convincing both to the individual and to his surrounding society, initiation requires a culture whose relationship with death is not simply one of opposition, a culture which does not view death as the body's greatest pathology, but which also sees it as an experience of the soul's transformation.[3] Initiation calls for a culture which does not seek to negate death, which doesn't see it as a finality, but for a culture able to symbolically appreciate death as a beginning.[4] The type of society in which initiation played an institutional role was a society in which death itself had an official position. It is no accident that both of these conditions have disappeared together.

If regenerative experiences are to be granted an official capacity within a society, the society in question must be a relatively simple one in which an individual's life can easily be separated from that of his neighbors. It must also be possible to isolate, with relative ease, the various phases of life from each other. The initiate is reborn, but he remains in this world where he must go on eating and living, and to a certain extent socializing—where he must remain tied to his mundane duties and commitments.

A modern complex society, generally speaking, offers relatively greater individual freedom, but also greatly increases the limits entailed by the individual's mundane existence. Does this society allow

---

2. Eliade defines this ancient procedure as a set of rites and oral teachings aimed at drastically altering the religious and social status of the individual undergoing initiation. The neophyte becomes, as it were, another person. Later in the same work, Eliade asserts that what initiation does in modern terms is put an end to the "natural man" and introduce the indifferentiated individual to culture. See Eliade, M., *Initiation, rites, sociétés secrètes*, Paris: Gallimard, 1959, pp. 12 and 20. See also Baudrillard, J., *L'échange symbolique et la mort*. Paris: Gallimard, 1976. For information on initiation as a bridge between the sacred and the profane, see Eliade's *The Sacred and the Profane*. New York: Harcourt Brace Jovanovich, 1968.

3. For psychological as opposed to medical discussion on the subject, see Hillman, J., *Suicide and the Soul*. Dallas: Spring, 1978.

4. The radical transformation of the concept of death in our culture has been the subject of many analyses, especially in France and the USA. See Aries, P., *Western Attitudes Towards Death From the Middle Ages to the Present*. Baltimore: Johns Hopkins University Press, 1974. Also, see my two articles on the topic, "Working Against Dorian Gray: Analysis and the Old," in *The Journal of Analytic Psychology*, vol. 28, I, 1983, pp 51-64, and "La pietra e la banana," in von Franz, Frey-Rohn, Jaffé, Zoja, *Incontri con la morte*. Milan: Raffaello Cortina, 1984.

an individual to radically alter his condition without setting off a series of contradictions that would alienate him from the world? The question is hard to answer, since the structure of modern life tends to eliminate possibilities of radical change. Ideological conversions, such as becoming a member of a political group, generally have few if any institutional characteristics, so it is hard to determine what their ramifications are in terms of the initiatory model.

Visible and institutionally recognized possibilities for renewal face, in our times, almost insuperable obstacles. A person often spends as much time studying for his profession as he later dedicates to it—thus radical changes of activity are from the very outset discouraged by the majority mentality. Contemporary economic structures, the need, for instance, to build one's credit by assuming debts, also tend to foster stasis in one's mode of living. Cultural factors discourage radical change in the actual material conditions of life and thus create a kind of psychological stasis, which from the point of view of fantasy leaves little room for imagining oneself in terms of renewal.

With the exception of the churches, whose official role is by and large decreasing, institutions tend towards practical results while relegating the problem of his own interior development to the individual. As mentioned above, institutions consequently do not address the problem of initiation, a problem which arises today as the return of an aspect of culture that has been repressed, as a need once satisfied but now denied by our official culture, and consequently manifested in occult or unconscious ways. Like most archetypal processes, initiation produces a ritual framework around itself. A group of "officiants" can thus quite easily form, held together by shared arcana, by the use of initiatory language, and by the celebration of rituals in common. Around the need for initiation, organizations are born, neither official nor conscious that they have at least partially an initiatory function. From this point of view, we can see how the repression of a need satisfied for thousands of years entails not only individual risks but also collective ones.

The latent need for secret groups and initiatory experiences can at times result in the formation of occult power structures, such as in terrorist groups, for example. It would be overly simplistic to interpret the initiatory aspect of these groups as mere expedients guaranteeing maximum efficiency and secrecy. The decisive element in the initiation into a terrorist group, for instance, often consists of the perpetration of a criminal act which cuts the initiate off from legal society and makes his bond with his colleagues concrete and real.

In general it is the occult structure which grows out of a need for esoterism, not the other way around. The need for esoterism seems to be present even when it is not understood, even in the "secrecy" games of children. Secret rituals inherently call for respect and solemnity, and aside from their functional aspect, they are fascinating and arouse the curiosity of outsiders.

Both literature and cinema have exploited this theme, drawing not so much on the public's political interests as on its latent curiosity for the hidden, for the secrecy of ritual. Though more or less indifferent to the ideological particuliarities of terrorist groups, the public at large responds to depictions of them with a mixture of horror and fascinated curiosity.

An analysis of the need for esoterism is of interest to us as we attempt to understand the phenomenon of drug addiction. From the point of view of the unconscious, turning to drugs can be understood as an attempt at a kind of initiation defective in its basic premise because of a lack of awareness. The "true" process of initiation—an initiation that fulfills the initiate's underlying psychic needs—can be encapsulated in three distinct phases.

First, the situation at the outset is one that must be transcended because of its meaninglessness. In order to transcend his meaningless state of existence, the adolescent in a primitive society entrusted himself to the initiatory process, which imbued him with a complete, adult identity. Similarly, the individual in our own society—passive, lost, condemned to a state of mere consumerism—secretly dreams of transforming himself into a separate, creative adult, no longer bound to consumerism.

Second, initiatory death. This phase entails a renunciation of the world, the rejection of one's previous identity, and the withdrawal of the libido from its habitual direction (in our society, this consists in above all refraining from consumerist behavior).

Third, initiatory rebirth, made psychologically easier by sharing the experience with others and by ritual—for instance, the controlled consumption of drugs. (The fantasy of control almost always exists in young drug users, but is for the most part only possible within the cultural context of certain primitive societies).

Our society's drug users fail to accomplish this process not so much because of how they take drugs (which is more often than not uncontrolled than controlled), but because they entirely omit the second phase, initiatory death. They are from the very outset intoxicated, not with a particular substance, but with the very consumerism they wish to negate—but consumerism does not allow for renunciation, or depression, or psychic voids of any kind. What today's users lack is the interior space which, together with external rituals, serves to contain the experience of renewal.

It might have been better, in the interest of a more rigorous analysis and in order to introduce new concepts, to use the term *drug initiation* instead of *drug addiction*. The actual object of our investigation is the fantasy, unconscious or not, that equates the *encounter* with a drug with the encountering of a new world and a new life—without the degeneration entailed by remaining in that drug-induced world. The term "drug initiate" would thus refer to that hypothetical individual who doesn't *abuse* drugs, but who *uses* them as a means of satisfying his innate, archetypal need for initiation. Because of psychic factors outlined in the following chapters, the contemporary drug user is never able to fully renounce the demands of his ego, a vital element in his "initiatory death." We will consequently employ the terms "drug user" or "drug addict," which today connote tremendous psychic and physical suffering, only because the "drug initiate" is a concept, a hypothetical ideal impossible to achieve in context of our consumerist culture. Under ideal conditions, were all drug users "drug initiates," the initial moment (taking a drug) would correspond to the initiatory moment (achieving transcendence). As we will see in the following chapters, drug consumption in so-called primitive societies is often quantitatively limited and qualitatively sheltered from the abuse of individual pathologies.

The psychological interpretation we are proposing, the initiatory moment—not to be confused with the initial moment—is what is of real importance. If, in fact, the expectations lying beneath the initiatory moment are archetypal, then they never die but rather continue to recur both as collective manifestations and individual pathologies. This study is not directed at the field of psychopathology, but is rather an investigation of the unconscious models which lead one to drugs despite the dangers involved. The investigation is not without clinical interest, even though it concentrates on the overall phenomenon rather than on the individual case of drug addiction.

What are the unconscious urges that lead a person into the vicious circle of addiction? Certainly, a degree of curiosity is involved. If we keep in mind that our bodies today have a very great tolerance for foreign substances, then we can imagine that this curiosity—this unconscious expectation—is not easily repressed, and that even when an apparently *physical* vicious circle of dependence is finally established, that the curiosity is some unrecognized psychological factor fueling the dependence itself. Our thesis is that the act of turning to drugs activates certain archetypal expectations which do not diminish as physical addiction sets in.

It should be noted that initiation and the process of drug use both adhere to similar archaic unconscious models, an argument important in and of itself. I am not attempting to address the question as to whether this potential model might have developed phylogenetically or if it were present *ab origine*. We cannot say that we have found a particular myth or specific god metaphoric of initiation or drug addiction. Initiation, and the use of drugs which unconsciously echoes its structure, is fundamentally an archetypal process, bi-polar like all archetypal themes (based on the opposition of life and death) and therefore impossible to personify, since it potentially belongs to any type of personality. Initiation assumes mythic forms in every culture, as do all solemn events, but it does not derive from one myth valid for all peoples. For each people, initiation is a means of returning mythic life to the commonality, and of conferring upon the individual a certain state of grace mere biological birth cannot provide.

CHAPTER 2

REFLECTIONS ON THE PROBLEM

The Drug Addict and Analysis

In order to understand the various aspects of drug addiction we are attempting to approach through the model of initiation, we must proceed step by step through the elements that led us to reflect on the problem in the first place.

My first contact with drug addicts was in context of my psychotherapeutic practice, where I was struck by the fact that therapy with such patients is especially difficult and often frustrating. My Jungian training led me to question to what degree the drug addict was acting out of habits acquired from his surroundings, to what degree urges potentially common to all mankind were at play, and if the addiction were activating these rather than creating them. I also questioned to what extent one could see in these urges, in these archetypal patterns, not just a negative escape but also a positive attempt at self-affirmation, even though that attempt often goes awry and degenerates.

On beginning therapy with a drug addict, one immediately senses that this patient will be more difficult than most, or more exactly, that his treatment will entail difficulties not encountered with other patients. One naturally turns to colleagues and to the literature for

9

help, but it is surprising to discover that analysts of all schools have an extremely low number of drug addicts in therapy, and that analytic literature on the subject is meager. The fact is amazing given that drug addiction almost automatically entails great psychic suffering, which every school of depth psychology is bound by duty to address. The fact is all the more striking in light of the dimensions the problem has assumed in modern society.

Although the situation is anything but flattering to analysts in general, their reluctance to deal with the problem is in some respects understandable. The fact is that the number of successes achieved in the psychotherapy of drug addicts is much less than that achieved in the treatment of other psychic disorders. If this fact is checked statistically over a period of time (short-term remissions are frequent and misleading), the number of successes in proportion to the number undergoing therapy is very low—but we must wonder if this evaluation is truly valid.

In the first place, the concept of *cure,* often inappropriately borrowed from medical terminology, must be examined. The values and aims of medicine are different from those of analysis—in the case of drug addiction, for instance, medicine will seek to overcome a state of intoxication, and its goal will be to heal battered organs. Depth psychology, on the other hand, strives to resolve certain contradictions and unconscious psychic sufferings. Some of this psychic suffering can obviously be alleviated without the circle of addiction necessarily being broken at the same time. In other words, the use of a toxic substance is for medicine in itself an evil, while for depth psychology it represents a symptom which may become chronic and which may exist independently of its "cause"—a psychic disturbance whose nature, development, and existence are very hard to verify.

The second element affecting the therapy of drug addicts is linked to the question of *motivation.* Organic medical treatment can be performed on an unwilling and uncooperative person, whereas by definition analytic therapy can only really be conducted given deep personal motivation on the patient's part.[1] This is where one encounters problems in treating drug addicts. The desire to carry through

1. Several colleagues and I have published a brief collection of essays on this problem. See *Perché si va in analisi.* Milan: Formichiere, 1977.

with analysis is often imposed from outside rather than being internal and truly psychological; treatment is imposed on the drug addict when, at the peak of an acute phase, he shows definite signs of asocial behavior. When the storm is over, and perhaps the first results of therapy obtained, this pressure eases and the patient resumes his life just as before.

For a while during therapy the patient will be drunk on good intentions and pleasant feelings. The ego of the drug addict seems in fact to be overwhelmed not only by the physical effects of his habit, but also by all sorts of intense and primitive emotions similar to those aroused by the drug he takes, since both the drug and the therapy activate the same archetypal contents. The patient finds it important to see his analyst as an ally, someone who believes in his good intentions. This ally, then, is a partial external substitute for the solidity and compactness lacking in the patient's ego, an external screen upon which the patient can project self-esteem and self-confidence, and by so doing, perhaps retrieve these missing qualities.

The drug addict's behavior leads some therapists to believe that he is psychopathic, but this is not at all the case. He is rather oppressed by particularly weighty internal demands (what Freud refers to as the "sadism of the superego"), and so naturally he seeks a good external authority to replace the cruel internal one.

In the addict's cooperative stages, his good will, his candor, and his desire for redemption can be quite apparent, expressed with such openness and simplicity that the patient, who may not at first have been convinced of the genuineness of his own resolutions, ends up believing in them. At other times the addict will be extremely reticent and defensive, displaying an obvious unwillingness to confront his own unconscious motivations. The patient seeks above all an ally in the analyst, and simultaneously the alleviation of his own sense of guilt. Both the external "moralism" of society and the addict's internal guilt are directed at the symptoms of a problem (his pathological obsession with drugs) and not its underlying causes.

An additional factor complicating the problem of motivation in the drug addict is that his family is very often neurotic, and in a sense dependent on him for its own equilibrium. What is called "anti-psychiatry" has gone so far as identifying the family itself as the cause of much drug addiction. Even though the argument has lost favor in recent years, it should be credited for pointing out how a family often uses one of its members, the drug addict, to free itself of other responsibilities. The family, though not necessarily the cause of the problem, seems to play a role in its perpetuation. Were we speaking of a drinker, we would say that the family is more interested in his *drunkenness* than in his *alcoholism*.

When we attempt to evaluate the results of therapy performed on drug addicts, we should thus base our estimates not on the number coming in for analysis, but rather on the number who actually undertake it. Those not truly motivated should not be counted since they do not, after all, ever actually begin. Many addicts enter therapy expecting to be cured, or to be reassured, but in no way willing to question themselves. The most one can do in such cases is a sort of social work. The failure in obtaining lasting therapeutic results with drug addicts should not be attributed to the failure of an analysis that never even took place, but rather to the analyst's inability to recognize the ambiguity of his patient's motivations, which in practice can only really be clarified once therapy is actually undertaken. Therapy which starts off as an addict's search for a sympathetic ally may open up into positive transference, and in this context the patient may begin to really question himself and his motivations.

Practical sense is the most important element in evaluating the drug addict's motivations, since the necessary analytical work can often only be undertaken in a protected clinical environment,[2] an artificial environment not very conducive to the development of what we might call the patient's ideal motivation. This drawback is nevertheless outweighed by an important advantage. By placing together individuals who are all attempting to fight off their addiction, not only is a community spirit instilled, but also the atmosphere of a mystical group which exalts and mutually reinforces their attempts at reaching a common goal.

This method, relied upon by Alcoholics Anonymous as well as by other drug-therapy groups, supports our initial hypothesis: individual drug users are very prone to group phenomena. A group's code of

---

2. This opinion can also be found in Chapter Thirteen of Rosenfeld's *Psychotic States*, (London: Hogarth Press, 1965), which includes a survey of what literature exists on the subject.

behavior in the streets, for example the way its members acquire and take their drugs, seems to have not only a practical function but also a ritual one. Such behavior unconsciously recalls the ancient *rites of entrance* through which an individual was elevated into a more prestigious group or social class. Were today's drug abusers "initiatory" groups in the full sense of the word, they would have to anticipate, as a final stage, the individual's separation from the group itself. Both the approach to and movement away from the drug would have to be facilitated and strengthened by the group.

The ancient initiatory models are much more closely followed by clinical drug-therapy groups than by groups of drug users on the street (who, for reasons examined in later chapters, are trapped by their own consumerism). Not only do clinical groups develop particular rites of entrance analogous to those in primitive cultures, but they also facilitate the individual patient in his abandonment of the group through a *rite of exit or separation*, which is traditionally classified as a particular *rite of passage*.[3] Thus separation from the therapy group or the end of one's symbiotic relationship with drugs could both be seen in terms of initiatory stages. Compared with initiation into drug use, these phases are more difficult in that they complete the initiatory cycle and thus confront the individual with his own loneliness, but also grant him an infinitely greater self-awareness. In this light, perhaps we can understand why so many therapies based on detoxification end up in failure. It is impossible to simply eliminate a behavior without redirecting the patient towards a completely new dimension.

The difficulties involved in the therapy of drug addicts do not, however, prevent the situation from reversing during analysis—which is possible if the therapeutic encounter is a good one and if the relationship between patient and analyst is strong enough to both activate and contain the introversion the patient was not initially prepared to face. It can be equally important for the patient to come into contact with people waging the same battle, which in practical terms could mean the incorporation of a group approach into the analysis. The first phase in the process of freeing oneself of drugs may

3. See van Gennep, A., *Rites of Passage*. Chicago: University of Chicago Press, 1960.

even lie in transferring one's dependency onto the analyst or the
therapy group.

Above and beyond the considerations of *cure* and *motivation,*
another element to keep in mind in the therapy of drug addiction is
the economic one. Estimates made in Switzerland and West Germany
in the last decade indicate that every real addict costs society between
a million and a million and a half Deutschmarks or Swiss francs, which
translated into current dollar figures would mean well over several
hundred thousand per addict per year. In a society whose most
important values are expressed in economic terms, this is decidedly
a *negative investment.* In this sense, it does not seem correct to
say that the drug addict is someone who denies society's dominant
imperative to be an economic being. He is not absent from the
economic picture, but rather present in a destructive way.

I have more than once come across or heard tell of the paradoxical
attitude of a drug addict proudly announcing "I take drugs!" In such
cases it hardly seems adequate to view the addict's entrance into the
world of drugs as a *regression,* a rejection of one's personal identity
or social role. It should on the other hand be seen as an active, more
or less conscious choice on the addict's part to remedy his lack of
identity and role by assuming a clearly defined negative identity and
role.

A word about the concepts of identity and role is in order at this
point, since it is impossible to completely separate the psychological
view of drug addiction from the sociological one. By *identity* we mean
an internal psychological life-experience endowed with coherence
and continuity (the recognition that we are who we are, even though
that understanding can vary with time and place). By *role,* a sociological term, we refer to that external element corresponding to identity;
inevitably much less personal, it is how a society perceives the status
and function of one of its members. Neither identity nor role is
necessarily understood consciously by the individual it is attributed
to.

We should note that every identity and role is constructed through
a process of progressive refinement and differentiation, arising from
fundamental archetypal themes which are naturally much harder to
determine the more a person's identity has been concretized and the

more that roles in society have become specialized. In Jungian terms, however, there will always be a Hero archetype or a Great Mother archetype or any other archetype , though these archetypes can be more easily recognized in personality phases where a stable ego structure has not yet developed (because of youth) or where it wavers (because of psychic pathologies).[4]

The Negative Hero

As we mentioned in the first chapter, we are dealing with archetypal processes rather than with archetypal figures. Initiation is in fact a process once the province not only of a few individuals, but which could concern a whole population, or at least the male part of it. Now that we have begun to examine the unconscious attempt at initiation manifested in drug addiction, however, we must alter our original premise: at the root of the modern phenomenon of drug addiction one can generally sense the presence of a *personified archetypal reality known as the negative hero*.

The archetypal need to transcend one's present state at any cost, even when it entails the use of physically harmful substances, is especially strong in those who find themselves in a state of meaninglessness, lacking both a sense of identity and a precise societal role. In this sense it seems right to see the behavior of a drug addict who announces "I use drugs!" not only as an escape to some other world, but also as a naive and unconscious attempt at assuming an identity and role negatively defined by the current values of society. Drug addiction is not, as generally believed, an escape from society, but a desperate attempt to occupy a place in it. Insofar as the addict perceives that his family is revolving hypnotically around him and that society is judging his behavior as an attack on civic unity, he always remains *homo œconomicus* while playing out his societal role as the negative hero.

It is almost impossible for many young people to feel in any way useful in today's society. Why should we be so amazed that so many take drugs, and why should we interpret addiction as a regressive renunciation of the ego when the person making this choice is actually

4. See Neumann, Erich, *History and Origins of Consciousness*. Princeton: Princeton University Press, 1958.

seeking a few moments of heroic identity? The archaic necessity of identifying both heroes and enemies becomes concentrated in the addict's creeping sensation of living a kind of civil war between a minority faction, made up of angels of death, and a stronger majority of law-abiding citizens. The latter, however, seem to lack any identity of their own.

The efforts a person makes to become himself, to be conscious of and responsible for his own development and his own choices—or his ego's efforts in emerging from preconscious darkness—have all been expressed in various mythologies by the isolated hero struggling with enemies and dragons. From the archetypal point of view, this battle is metaphoric of every initial moment in psychological development, where the very existence of the ego is still at stake and its strengthening imperative. Thus the need for heroic experience or identification is felt most strongly as an individual is maturing.

The individual's struggles to affirm himself a place in society, carried out in the name of personal ambition or ideology, are determined by particularly rigid and pre-established guidelines which deprive the individual of a large part of his personal responsibility, or what was once considered as such. On the other hand, the main characteristic of the hero's battle in its purest and most archetypal form is the fact that he puts his very existence at stake, that he fights wholeheartedly to either win or die. But in our modern world, where every acrobat is assured of a safety net below him, such an experience has been relegated to the unconscious.

The alternative to dramatic victory is not dramatic defeat, but the flattening out of life into an insignificant existence governed by institutional organs. The ideal of our public institutions is to prevent almost all kinds of death; if someone refuses to eat, he should be force-fed. The elderly person afflicted with the ailments of age is hospitalized, since death, even natural death, has been gradually removed from the realm of normal physiology and now is assumed to be a sort of pathological occurence. If death is not faced personally and consciously, then psychic life suffers one of its worse mutilations. As Freud puts it in his *Thoughts for the Times on War and Death,* "Life is impoverished, it loses interest if the highest stake in the game of living, life itself, cannot be risked."

Any struggle still possible presupposes an involution of the heroic experience. The State has monopolized violence, depersonalized it, and denied it to the individual. The practice of duelling, even in its most ritualized and mitigated forms, has been completely banned. This was of course inevitable, but the situation is not without its psychological repercussions. Why is it that when we speak of duels, we qualify them as a barbarian custom? Perhaps the "barbarians" accepted a little bit of blood as a lesser evil in order to satisfy some psychological need—namely, that through the "judgement of God" the divinity itself (we would say "the archetypal reality") was directly expressed in the duellists' acts.

Our various chiefs of staff prepare machines able to shed oceans of blood in impersonal and deritualized duels, in the name of national or ideological values often abstractly determined at the negotiating table. The individual citizen is barred from taking part in the preparation of these mega-duels, which will never be able to stop at "the first draw of blood," nor to "make satisfaction," as the codes of chivalry used to say. Today, of course, the duel as a means of justice strikes us as absurd. It is not so easy to condemn, however, when we see it as a search for a solution considered just by all the parties involved, yet not imposed on them by an external authority. In psychological terms, the experience of justice should be a profound one, corresponding with archetypal urges. In current law, however, the penalty for duelling depends not on the violence of the act itself, but rather on the fact that a direct administration of justice has been perpetrated by those involved. What we must realize is that the duel is psychologically a very powerful phenomenon, especially in terms of its conflict with the State's conception of jurisprudence.

There appears to be a specific link between the modern conception of law and jurisprudence and our contemporary difficulty in living out archetypal experiences such as that of heroism. Neo-liberals hold the welfare state responsible for our society's neurasthenia and anxious inability to grant the individual responsibility, the final and most devastating results of the welfare system. One might well wonder whether this decline in societal vitality is in some way due not only to the socio-economics of the welfare state, but also to the philosophy of modern law, which guarantees certain rights to the individual and thus absolves him from fighting for them. In other words, the rational bases upon which the idea of the modern State is founded are not enough. Archetypal realities have a place alongside rational values, since rational values are incapable, on their own, of administering the economy of the psyche. Thus what was defined above as a decline in societal vitality could also be defined as an absence of archetypal resonance within society. A psychic experience that has no links with an archetypal theme does not vibrate with sufficient intensity to make it viable or to allow it much impact on the individual or collective psyche—the experience lacks a deeper echo.

In its attempts at being fair and objective, the administration of justice becomes highly rationalistic. This rational quality is of course necessary, but it works against the immediacy, the intensity, the "gut quality" of those feelings which make experiences *archetypal*. The law becomes more distant and impersonal, but the archetype, the interior law, must express itself personally. If a god "speaks," the primitive or the madman hears the voice and knows that it has spoken to him; instead of grasping a concept, he actually *hears* the voice. The height of emotional intensity in the search for justice was reached when the outcome of a duel coincided with the judgement of God; the archetype of the hero coincided with the archetype of higher justice, and the ego with the Self.

The direct personification of an archetype—when the individual ego identifies with a divine or mythical personage—is possible only in extreme cases. In most cases, an archetype is a projected personification, that is, experienced in the form of an external representative separate from the individual himself. The fact that the duel was expected to deal justice less abstractly and more personally made the archetypal experience more immediate, even for the non-combattants, since they could project their own image of justice onto the duellist they favored.

Archetypal needs tend to resist time and cultural evolution. An archetypal fantasy, something completely foreign to the juridical structures of modern society, often survives as a more or less serious form of paranoia. A commoner, for instance, would once risk being run over by a nobleman's carriage just to hand him some appeal or

request, since the nobleman coincided with the commoner's archetypal idea of justice. Many individuals who suffer some injustice today
often entertain the fantasy that theirs is not a technical or legal problem, but a personal one. If some *personage,* authoritative, archetypal,
and duly idealized, would just see to the problem *personally*, then
"everything will be alright."

The mass media need the greatest possible unconscious participation from the public, and thus prefer to provide us with archetypal
themes rather than concepts. Understanding the public's potential
fascination with archetypal personifications, they turn well-known
public figures into stars or demi-gods. Archetypal experiences are
often dangerously antithetical to rationality and objectivity, though
in certain cases archetypal projections can be harmless enough—
identification through projection with John Lennon is naive, but far
less dangerous than the same sort of identification with, say, Hitler.
Otherwise we run the risk of being exposed to the recurrence, in
an undifferentiated, unconscious, and pathological way, of contents
repressed from consciousness.

In 1957, in his *Commentary on "The Secret of the Golden Flower,"*
Jung outlines the range of personified archetypes in context of the
phenomenology of religion:[5]

> Many of the earlier gods developed from "persons" into per-
> sonified ideas, and finally into abstract ideas. Activated uncon-
> scious contents always appear at first as projections upon the
> outside world, but in the course of mental development they
> are gradually assimilated by consciousness and reshaped into
> conscious ideas that then forfeit their originally autonomous and
> personal character. As we know, some of the old gods have
> become, via astrology, nothing more than descriptive attributes
> (martial, jovial, saturnine, erotic, logical, lunatic, and so on). (¶49)

Jung continues several paragraphs later[6]:

> We [Europeans] think we can congratulate ourselves on already
> having reached such a pinnacle of clarity, imagining that we have
> left all these phantasmal gods far behind. But what we have left
> behind are only verbal spectres, not the psychic facts that were

5. Jung, C.G., *Commentary on "The Secret of the Golden Flower,"* in *Collected Works*, vol.
13. Princeton: Princeton University Press, 1976.
   6. *Ibid.*

responsible for the birth of the gods. We are still as much possessed by autonomous psychic contents as if they were Olym-
pians. Today they are called phobias, obsessions, and so forth; in
a word, neurotic symptoms. The gods have become diseases;
Zeus no longer rules Olympus but rather the solar plexus, and
produces curious specimens for the doctor's consulting room,
or disorders the brains of politicians and journalists who unwit-
tingly let loose psychic epidemics on the world. [¶54]

This process of "emptying the heavens" does not mean that
archetypal personages have disappeared completely, but rather that
it is no longer possible to project them in the ancient manner.
Like the instincts, archetypes can only be repressed. As individual
unconscious interior forces, they can easily be projected onto
whatever appears "lofty" to us, whatever satisfies our need to
believe—in today's world, philosophies or ideologies rather than
traditional divinities. Jung recognized the necessity of answering
this fundamental need, but he also expressed a lack of trust
in these modern answers, considering them too conceptual and
rationalistic. They end up substituting for religions, but are condemned to an ephemeral and neurotic existence—neurotic because
they actually function as religions without being aware of the fact,
and ephemeral because they lack symbolic expressiveness, or as
we said earlier, archetypal resonance.

Jung has been accused of reactionism because of these positions,
but he was in reality anti-positivist and anti-academic. Having no
illusions about world-views offering general solutions to life, he believed in the possibility of deepening the individual's psychological
awareness and responsibility. The Jungian point of view, far from
being merely a reactionary denial of modern ideologies, offers us a
chance of correcting the psychological limits imposed by them.

In *Archetypes of the Collective Unconscious* (*Collected Works*, vol
IX, ¶ 22), Jung criticizes the rarified and conceptualized atmosphere
of Protestant theology, as well as its obvious symbolic poverty when
compared with Catholicism. Jung's diagnosis has many points in common with the works of Max Weber, who analyzed the process of
"disenchantment" (*Entzauberung*) of the modern world and considered Protestantism its prime expression. The destruction of the old

symbolic and magical world is as radical in its scope as the transformation of libido from an unconscious autonomous process into controlled and deliberate will. Our modern capitalist and technological
world, a product of rationalism, is not beyond the reach of primordial
archetypal influence and stimulation. The drunkenness of paganism
was, through fascism, reproduced most intensely in the overly disen-
chanted homeland of Luther, where the collective had long since
grown away from personified images and was therefore most unprepared to face archetypal experiences. In Italy, on the other hand,
fascism was less profound because the survival of magical beliefs,
Catholic ritual, and the proliferation of saints all functioned to keep
the connection with the chthonic pagan world from being severed.

Progressive thinkers have all too often taken an interest in the
mythological and psychological aspects of political movements only
when it was relatively late, when they finally understood that fascism
was able to mobilize not only those seeking material gain, but also a
large part of the population left without myths as well. This evaluation
has been stressed in many recent historical studies of fascism and
national socialism,[7] which have largely reevaluated the symbolic and
ritual elements—as opposed to abstract doctrine—of fascist movements, and which have underscored the charismatic and unifying
function of ideology personified in a leader.

The evolution of this type of historical analysis is of great interest
to the psychologist. At the end of World War II, studies of fascism were
more schematic, less psychological, and more intent on exorcising
fascism by underscoring the differences between it and the victorious
world-views, either liberal-capitalist or Marxist. This approach—in
which the observer places himself "completely outside" (using political categories lacking in psychological insight)—is redolent of the
Eurocentrism with which the very first ethnological studies were
carried out in the last century. European culture had only just entered
its modern era, yet it viewed still-archaic and pagan cultures as though
they were something from another planet. Today, however, ethnology
admits that there are many aspects of archaic, magic, and pagan man

7. I am referring to the works of Renza de Felice and George L. Moss.

still present in us, and we have learned to identify their traces. Our collective psychic defense system makes the situation we have only just grown out of seem incomprehensible at first; only with the passing of time is it possible to see how it lives on in us.

In much the same way, it took time for us to realize that fascism is in part a psychological potential in all of us, a realization possible only because of the distance between us and historical fascism. Since World War II, dictatorships in some way similar to fascism no longer seek to mobilize their masses, but rather to demobilize them—as seen in their abandonment of fascist liturgy and the symbolic participation exploited so well by Hitler. From the point of view of modern histori- ography, South American authoritarian regimes, Spain under Franco, and so on, are reactionary and conservative, but not truly fascist. In our own terminology, we could say that these dictatorships and fascist movements have not managed (or they have not tried) to inject themselves into the archetypal vacuum of modern society, nor to use it to disseminate their message.

The ability to evoke unsatisfied archetypal urges is thus still almost exclusively the domain of historical fascism and its anti-bourgeois roots. As a counterpoint to the "disenchantment" of the modern world, which is still being exploited by leftist movements, fascism could provide the hypnotic attraction of heroic roles—roles few people still believed in, but for which many more people longed. It should be noted that the heroism introduced by historical fascism was so subjected to the needs of the substantially modernized European nations that the result was a distortion, or rather a negation, of the original heroic spirit. Thus Hitler's "heroic" destruction of Germany was prevented, out of national interest, from ever taking place. The fascist movements in fact strove for concrete results in line with a specific concept of national interests, a positivism that does not correspond to the spirit of traditional heroic ethics, which is generally not interested in achieving visible results. The archetypal heroic real- ity is represented in this ethic, not in the utilitarianism later imposed on it.

Besides being over-functionalized, the heroic canon was artificially extended by fascism to include the masses. In 1936, on the eve of war, Johan Huizinga noted that fascism tried to exalt but generalize the distinction of "hero"—usually reserved for exceptional figures, and even then only attributed posthumously—in order to oblige the masses not to behave exceptionally, but simply to carry out orders.[8] As Huizinga notes in *In the Shadow of Tomorrow*, " . . . the concept of 'hero' underwent a shocking upheaval which deprived it of its more intimate meaning." The category of the hero, always associated with something personal and exceptional, eventually became devalued.

Fascist movements exploited a potential heroic need in order to recruit members, promising adventure and opportunities for profit. The attraction of profit should not be overestimated, however, since the recruitment was irrational in many respects, attracting even those who had little or nothing to gain and everything to lose; it attracted those driven by a deep urge not to amass, but to self-destruction. This aspect, as mentioned above, became stronger during the fall of fascism.

With the rise and defeat of fascism, we could say that the final elimination of the positive heroic spirit was hastened. It would be more correct, however, to say that negation is something ingrained in fascism itself, in its range of primarily destructive heroes, surrounded by skulls and symbols of death.

We thus have a more definite confirmation of something already evident in our discussion on the duel: the disappearance, during the recent course of history, of the possibility for individual struggle endowed with risk and responsibility, and capable of creating (in the purest cases, such as that of Odysseus) its own rules and its own plane of action. Those movements seeking to revive the heroic experience find themselves in conflict with a cultural anachronism, with types of behavior that are less heroic than primitive or horde-like, and all due to the fact that the movements are no longer able to relegate meaningful conflicts—because of their inherent complexity and interdependence—to the individual's own personal responsibility.

True heroic sentiment does not allow the subjection of the individual to collective norms (even though these have existed in every period in history) nor does it accept rational and objective goals

8. Huizinga, Johan, *In the Shadow of Tomorrow*. London: Heinemann, 1936.

and methods. As a result, the heroic sentiment is repressed by the collective, which accepts the loss but sinks into the dullness of antiheroic predictability, where individuality entails irrationalism or asocial behavior.

Traditional heroism is repressed or is primordially and unconsciously satisfied by the experiences of the destroyer-hero. Odysseys survive in the form of space travel, but in reality this is an immense "rational" collective undertaking which cannot be personified since it is carried out primarily by machines. It is no longer possible to discover other continents, but it would be very easy to destroy those already known. Thus it is no accident that in many political thrillers, which often express popular unconscious fantasies, this destruction is portrayed as the work, or the revenge, of an *individual* in the grip of destructive madness.

When an archetype is repressed, it tends to resurface ever more irrationally (since it is polarized as an antagonist of the ego, of consciousness), more primordially and schematically, and eventually merges with other repressions—evil, destructiveness, and the archetype of the shadow. The process is similar to what happened in our culture when it exaggerated its denial of the feminine, for then the witch-hunts, described by Jules Michelet and others, flared out of control. As mentioned above, the same holds true for death, which from many points of view is the most extensive repressed area of our time.

The inevitability of the death-archetype emerging in uncontrolled and irrational forms is somewhat mitigated by the fact that in the last few years death has become the object of a good deal of cultural and physiological research. And yet the very success of these books and studies allows us to see, once again, that the mere evocation of an archetype arouses emotions. The public is not so much in need of specialized studies as it is of a chance to participate fully in a total confrontation, like that between death and a living person, something once provided by rites and rituals. The mysticism and liturgy of fascism, though including some purely political aspects, reintroduced modernized versions of the ancients' cult of the dead.

Albeit in a naive, unconscious, and undifferentiated way, fascism in fact often did represent a neglected psychological element—the irrationality of the archetypal realities repressed by the rapid advance of a rationalist culture. This opposition is evident in an incident at the University of Salamanca on October 12, 1936. Miguel de Unamuno's opening lecture was interrupted by groups of Francoists shouting, "Down with intellectuals! Long live death!"

From the moment historical fascism was defeated, the archetypal realities linked to death and heroism have appeared on a more limited psychological plane. No longer subject to political and cultural forms codified enough to allow for their expression, these archetypal realities find an unconscious outlet in the form the negative hero. The worlds of drugs, or gun-smuggling, or terrorism, appear to be the heirs of those archetypal realities already evoked by fascism.

CHAPTER 3

ARCHETYPAL FANTASIES
UNDERLYING DRUG ADDICTION

In this chapter, we will attempt to trace the modern phenomenon of drug use back to the ancient need for renewal through initiatory experiences. Couldn't the use of drugs, in terms of collective psychology, be linked with other archetypal needs? For example, might it not be a manifestation of the collective shadow, of that psychic element repressed into the unconscious by collective morality, but which cannot be eliminated completely simply *because* it is archetypal?

The equation of drug use with a violation of *moral* standards seems to be a very recent phenomenon, dictated by the structure of Western culture and its typical concerns with an infantile conception of transgression. It is much more fruitful to examine the problem archetypally, in terms of both its inner motivations and its various external manifestations, than to examine it ethically. The connection between drug consumption and immorality begins to disintegrate as soon as we consider the etymology of the words used to describe the phenomenon in European languages.[1]

1. The etymological references have been drawn from: Devoto, G., *Avviamento alla etimologia italiana*. Milan: Mondadori, 1979; *Duden Etymologie*. Mannheim: Mannheim Bibliographi-

27

First of all, we should note that when we use the term *drug* today, we mean not only a psychoactive substance, but also one whose use meets with sociocultural limitations. Thus although the alcoholic is technically considered an addict, alcohol itself is not generally thought of as a drug. English, as well as the four main Latin languages, Italian, French, Spanish, and Portugese, all use the word "drug," which comes from a clear and univocal root. Germanic languages also have other words ("addiction" and "craving" in English, *Sucht* in German) which express better than Latinate words (such as the Italian *dipendenza*) the largely archetypal relationship between a drug and an individual. It is interesting to note from the etymology of the words themselves that *substances as such* have no negative connotations, while the *relationship* between them and their users becomes increasingly negative with the passage of time.

The Greek *oinos* and the Latin *vinum*, both from the same non-Indo European root, have spread into all languages, almost always as descriptive words with no ethical implications. In Ancient Greece, wine was often referred to as *pharmakon,* which as we know can have either positive or negative connotations. The term "alcohol" comes from the Arabic *al-kuhl*, meaning "a fine, dry powder," and was introduced to Europe through alchemical works (Paracelsus uses the expression *alcohol vini* to mean "the essence of wine"). The absence of negative connotations in the word alcohol is all the more surprising given that it comes from a culture which, unlike our own, has always condemned the use of the substance. Thus alcohol, one of the very few unexotic drugs in our culture, has had for centuries an exotic (and esoteric) name. In later chapters we will attempt to understand why drugs are almost inevitably linked with the exotic and the esoteric.

The term "drug," which first appeared in the early spice trade, is derived from the Dutch *droog* ("dry goods") and similarly lacks negative connotations, as do the names of many specific drugs such as opium, which comes from the Greek *opos*, the juice of a plant.

sches Institut, 1963; *Shorter Oxford English Dictionary*. Oxford: Oxford University Press, 1933; *The Heritage Illustrated Dictionary of the English Language*. New York: William Morris, 1973; Danzat, Dubois, and Mitterand, *Nouveau dictionnaire etymologique*. Paris: Larousse, 1964; Ernout, A., and Meillet, A., *Dictionnaire etymologique de la langue latine*. Paris: Klinckseick, 1968; *The Oxford Dictionary of English Etymology*. Oxford: Oxford University Press, 1966.

The terms indicating addiction, however, do have many negative connotations, but it was only with time that these words became increasingly associated with the substance itself. *Sucht* comes from Old German and Gothic and has always meant "illness." Today, however, it refers to drug addiction in general. The word "addict" appears in England around the sixteenth century, but comes from the Latin *addictus*, "handed over (to someone) as a slave." "Addiction" thus originally meant giving oneself over, but little by little the meaning became connected with the use of drugs. A similar etymological evolution took place with the verb "to crave," which comes to us from the Old Norse verb for "to ask or demand intensely."

The evolution of the German term *Rausch*[2] is still more representative of this trend. In the sixteenth century the term meant "drunkenness," but only in more recent times has the compound form *Rausch-gift* appeared (*Gift* means "poison"), meaning a stupefying substance. The term "stupefying" appears in Latinate languages, and to a lesser extent in English, as an adjective, and more recently as a noun. It originally did not have a necessarily negative connotation—the Latin verb *stupeo* can either refer to a passive state of vacuity or to a feeling of admiration and wonder.

We are beginning to discover the outline of an unconscious collective paradigm or of a possible archetypal framework. Etymologically speaking, "addiction" is a phenomenon not automatically connected with *substances,* but with the ultimate corruption of substances by those who expect archetypal, magical, ritual, and esoteric results from them. One gives oneself over to a substance which comes from afar and, in the expectation of the user, is supposed to carry one far away. That the substance comes from exotic countries that have maintained their rites and folklore is no accident, nor is the fact that the substance bears an exotic name even if it is produced locally (alcohol, for example).

In his introduction to Freud's *Cocaine Papers,* James Hillman refers to the imaginative power of "exotic" drugs:[3]

2. An interesting thing about the word *Rausch* and its antonym *Nuchternheit* (sobriety) is that the latter, which apparently refers to a state of clarity and lucidity, in fact is derived from the Latin *nocturnus* and thus originally entailed darkness and silence. See Mattenklott, G., *Der ubersinnliche Leib*. Hamburg: Reibek, 1982, p. 211 ff.

3. Freud, Sigmund, *The Cocaine Papers*. James Hillman, ed. Vienna: Dunquin Press, 1963, p. vi.

Though these substances are, for the most part, new compounds, the hopes they carry are old. All periods of history and all cultures show the consumption of toxic substances for the purpose of altering perception and emotion. Alcohol in the Christian West and hashish in the Muslim East are examples. But when the substances are not native, when they come from far places and exotic peoples—as spices from Eastern islands, tobacco from the new world, rauwolfia from India, etc.—they would seem to be charged with a special significance. Coca from Peru fits this pattern.

This pattern in traditional symbolism is represented as the "healing elixir" or "herb of immortality," brought back from a remote land, bearing an alien name, processed in a special way, distributed ritualistically, and potent even in minute quantities. Its negative effects can be toxic especially when ingested by those not ripe for it. Its positive effects include healing, rejuvenation, and liberation. These ideas, carried by myth and ceremony, are so universal that we must consider the possibility that we are being confronted with an archetypal phenomenon (p. vi).

The passage is worth noting since it contains some observations that confirm the hypothesis of an archetypal relationship between our psychic needs and our unconscious fascination with the world of drugs. Hillman's observations provide the basis of another hypothesis, that the "herb of immortality," the exotic drug, is spontaneously associated by our unconscious archetypal fantasy with initiatory processes and the formation of esoteric communities. This hypothesis is supported by the fact that the substance itself, like the chosen group or the initiatory rite, is veiled in mystery, hinting at the possibility of immortality (of the spirit), and a greater and more ancient wisdom analogous to that of the wondrous East, from where the substance comes. Unlike alcohol, which is profane, familiar, and readily available, the exotic drug is a metaphor for wisdom and psychic experience revealed only to the chosen few.

Thus far we have concentrated on the substance itself, not on the actual process of addiction. Before we do so, we should schematize the process in order to distinguish its psychological motivations from its purely physical ones. The scheme breaks down into three main components:

First, and varying in importance with the relative potency of the drug, there appears to be a physical, organic habit formation in the user.

Second, there develops a psychological habit which tends to transform itself into a kind of conditioning, especially when individual modes of behavior are reinforced by a group, and vice-versa.

Third, the presence of a parareligious element (we might also define this element as the "sacred") which unlike the other two elements is neither acquired nor culturally conditioned, but is rather an archetypal tendency. This element would be responsible for the spontaneous formation of rituals and for the drug addict's tendency towards esoterism.

The distinction between the first and the second of the three elements is relatively clear. Unlike in the past, we know today that the organic element in habit formation is greatly overestimated and that, from the biological point of view, breaking a habit is almost always possible, even in the case of "heavy" drugs.

The distinction between the second and third elements is less obvious, and this is partly due to the fact that the individual involved is generally conscious of the second (the conditioning factor) but not of the third (the user's striving for the sacred). The fact that the third element is the least conscious explains to some extent why most other schematizations of drug addiction tend to be reductive, concentrating only on its physical and conditioned aspects. As we can see from the ineffectiveness of most drug treatment programs, the problem of addiction is not easily conducive to such reductive terms.

We occasionally find a drug addict who has managed to free himself of the first two elements (roughly speaking, physical intoxication and obsessive pathology) by apparently having found in himself those new values he previously sought externally. He seems to alter his own world view, but when this view is not sufficiently altered, we begin to see the former addict falling into another dependence, either on a new substance or on another pathological behavior—fanatic adherence to a religious sect, compulsive eating, and so on. Even membership in Alcoholics Anonymous, certainly one of the most effective programs against alcoholism, influences the individual by promoting the acritical, unconditional participation characteristic of sacred rites.

The analyst, or at least not the Jungian analyst, cannot ignore the third element in our schematization, since his work is not so much predicated on the elimination of pathologies as on a full appreciation of their broader perspective, on the unconscious creative finality of addiction. This third element is not just an interpretive tool, but also a readily perceivable reality. At times, drug addiction can be entirely a function of the third element, the first two having little or no effect on the addict, a situation clearly exemplified in Freud's "addiction" to cocaine. In Hillman's words,

> Freud was never in the grip of the drug as a drug, but he seems to have been, during this period, under the spell of an archetypal factor constellated by the drug.[4]

The facts were later to reveal that Freud was not attempting to express unconscious aspects of himself through the particular sensations produced by cocaine, but through psychological research considered scientific: scientific truth was in fact the "sacred" element he was seeking. If we need an example closer to our own times, we need only ask how many of the young people who turned to hallucinogens in the last twenty years did so in search of hedonistic satisfaction, and how many did so because they were looking for a parareligious experience. Fortunately for them, the substances which typically produce a "metaphysical" experience rather than distorted physical sensations are those least likely to be physically addictive.

In order to examine this third element in more practical terms, we shall later study the case of an analysand who actually based his own addiction on a magical-religious ritual so as to better re-establish contact with a world he had experienced in his childhood imagination. What is unusual about his story is that he spontaneously discovered a way to take drugs without any help or suggestions from his environment. He gradually built up a series of rituals analogous to those of primitive cultures unknown to him. This leads us to hypothesize that the tendency to use drugs is not closely linked to specific environmental influences, but rather emanates from that "area" of the unconscious out of which autonomous realities can emerge independently of consciousness, personal history, or cultural milieu.

4. *Ibid.*, p. vii.

CHAPTER 4

DRUGS AND SOCIETY

Recourse to Drugs as a Collective Psychological Need

The initiatory model has provided us with some ideas useful in trying to understand the world of drugs in terms of archetypal fantasies and symbolic formations. We have already analyzed those creative and innovative aspects metaphorized by a drug's distant origins. This exotic quality fascinates Westerners in particular, but not exclusively. Opium, a drug common in Southeast Asia, was actually introduced from the Middle East. Wherever they appear, drugs generally function as messengers from "another world," an objective geographical projection of the very lively unconscious world activated by them. This internal world is a facet of our psychic life which the limited scope of everyday life does not allow us to actually touch, but which can, through the mediation of the "appropriate" powers, to a certain extent be revealed to us.

Ethnology, cultural anthropology, and history have taught us that a certain amount of drug use has always existed, and generally becomes accentuated when a society feels itself in a state of crisis.[1] In the most

1. For a general overview of the link between socio-cultural transformation and increased drug use, see the *UNESCO Courier*, Year XXV, January 1, 1982.

33

dramatic cases, the introduction of and struggle against a drug occurs when an entire culture is collapsing, usually because of the arrival of European "efficiency" and mercantile frenzy. Autochthonous cultures struggle to balance the dynamic of the ego and unconscious, of rationality and magic or fantasy. The arrival of the Europeans upsets this balance, separating the two poles and irreconcilably opposing them. The rational pole is monopolized by the European, while the mute and helpless native has no choice but to move further and further away in the direction of the primordial unconscious. Thus the American Indians who fought the alcohol merchants and the Chinese who waged the Opium Wars were doomed from the start—not simply because the U.S. Government or the British Crown were militarily unbeatable, but because their own countrymen, Indian or Chinese, were already lost to alcohol or opium.

In context of a relatively stable culture, moments of crisis similarly tend to increase collective drug consumption, which in turn results in an increase of legal prohibitions against the drug. Prohibitions, however, far from stamping out the use of a given drug (one need only think of the Great Prohibition of 1919-1932), make its use more guarded and intensify the bonds formed among its users, as well as accenting the initiatory and esoteric features of user-groups themselves.

The formation of distinct sub-cultures, each with its own language and ethical code, is almost unavoidable. The most obvious reason is juridical and sociological, for it is clear that prohibition fosters the formation of secret sects as a form of self-defense—yet this explanation is reductive in that it neglects the psychology of the unconscious and limits itself to an ethical, transgressive view of the question. The explanation does not give adequate weight to the inherently reassuring and excitant role played by the magic and ritual of esoteric language, almost as if the use of a drug activates the need for it—a need which tends to survive even after a drug becomes legalized, or at least decriminalized.

It would therefore seem that the rise of a subculture with all of its ritual is necessary for reasons other than the simple need to unite in the face of legal opposition. One reason is that very few individuals are capable of confronting profound experiences by themselves; in times of collective crisis, innovative experience must often be collective as well. What we in the last chapter termed our "third element" of addiction can help us understand the birth of subcultures—unlike the first element (biological dependence) and the second (pathological dependence), both of which are factors in individual rather than collective addiction. While the Freudian *personalistic* orientation of depth psychology might have more precise clinical concepts at its disposal, it nevertheless sees the problem from a much narrower angle than the Jungian perspective, which with its concepts of collective conscious and unconscious is more directly suited to cultural analyses.

How then are we to interpret the fact that drug use tends to increase when a particular culture is in crisis, and that legal prohibitions actually accentuate the esoteric and initiatory aspects of consumption? A juridical interpretation would see esoterism as an attempt to side-step a legal constraint; Freudian psychology would focus on the individual aspects of the problem. A Jungian interpretation, however, presumes that a basic need for renewal is being activated in the culture at large.

In order to better understand how initiation and drugs can be linked through archetypal fantasies, it would be useful, before moving on to more immediate problems, to discuss a myth from a relatively simple and isolated society. We can thus examine an archetypal theme in its purest possible form.

A myth is like a dream experienced at the cultural level—it tells us about the unconscious needs of a whole society. The influence of individuals in the formation of the myth is, by definition, marginal. We will examine a myth from the Arekuna culture (Central Guiana) as reported by Lévi-Strauss in *From Honey to Ashes*.[2] The simplicity of this particular myth and the fact that it is so foreign to European culture emphasize its universal and archetypal aspects while, above and beyond cultural specificity, underscoring its analogies with our own unconscious needs.

> The myth is entitled "The Origin of Tobacco and Other Magic Drugs," and opens with a child, who has led his four brothers into the forest where they come across some birds (djiadjia) (not

2. Lévi-Strauss, Claude, *From Honey to Ashes*. New York: Harper & Row, 1973.

identified) whose cry means "further, further!" The children have not eaten even though they have in fact brought some food along with them; they want to kill the birds, which allow the boys to come close without any difficulty. The boys, however, miss their target. Chasing their prey, the boys continue going further and further away and they finally end up on the plantation where the servants of Piai'man, the Lord of Tobacco, work. The servants are frightened by the arrows and they beg the children to be careful so as not to pierce their eyes. The birds change into human beings in such a way that the children accept them as parents and agree to live with them.

Piai'man however wants the children for himself, since the birds who had drawn them in there are his property too. He wants to make the children into witch-doctor healers and every day he administers some emetic drinks to them. The children are isolated in a small hut where the women cannot see them. They vomit into the water of a fall "to absorb its noise" and into a large piragua. After taking all kinds of mixtures prepared with bark and "the souls" of various trees, the children who have become very thin and have lost consciousness, receive the nasal vapors of tobacco juice and undergo the painful trial of having to pass some cords made of hair through their noses along the backs of their throats and then out of their mouths.

Towards the end of this *initiation* two of the children do something that they had been forbidden to do; they lose their eyes and are changed into nocturnal spirits. The other three become full-fledged witch doctors and grow old together with their Lord. When their Lord finally sends them back to their village, they are completely bald. Their parents have a hard time recognizing them. A young girl whom they desired finds them too old; irritated by this fact, they change her into stone and then change the members of their own families into Spirits. These are the Spirits that today make the tobacco of the witch doctor healers grow in just ten days, without it even having to be planted. There are three varieties of this tobacco. It is very strong.

In the myth, which according to Lévi-Strauss uses "tobacco juice" to refer to *all* narcotic drinks,[3] the heroes are a little boy and his four brothers. According to traditional numerical symbolism,[4] five is a

---

3. It should be remembered that tobacco juice is a relatively strong narcotic in equatorial South America. See Harner, M.J., ed., *Hallucinogens and Shamanism*. New York: Oxford University Press, 1973, p. 25.

4. The number-symbolism is drawn from standard dictionaries of symbols, especially Chevalier and Gheerbrant, *Dictionnaire des symboles*. Paris: Seghers, 1973.

balanced number; it is also a central and totalizing symbol of the complete man. Thus the story starts off on the right foot, so to speak, though the characters are uninitiated children and not adults. The children have provisions, but they prefer hunting birds for food. Symbolically, they are abandoning matter and physical life in order to search for something more elevated. Birds generally represent thoughts, fantasies, a tendency for spiritual activity and a search for higher forms of being. Placing such a quest before a purely material one is another initiatory prerequisite, and as expected it leads the children "off the beaten path."

The children then risk gouging out the eyes of Piai'man's servants with their arrows. The arrow is an image of particularly quick thoughts, but also of a destiny of death. Keeping both of these meanings in mind, we can read the action as a warning to those who turn to drugs not "with their hearts" but "with their minds," and who do so too hastily, aiming directly at their goal. This warning is especially applicable to Westerners, whose culture has been fundamentally warped by its need to set the most achievable and visible goals possible. In approaching the world of Piai'man, the world of drugs, haste and intellectual one-sidedness entail the risk of only partially "seeing," of being only barely conscious.

The birds which lead the children are actually Piai'man's servants. In other words, fantasies and misconceptions about drugs—that it is possible to try them only once, out of intellectual curiosity, without losing one's will power—are the product of a basic naiveté. The fantasies are, after all, the servants of Piai'man. It is an illusion to think that such fantasies arise from conscious reflection and obey its commands; they are present, archetypally, in the way that man looks at drugs, and more precisely, they are instruments of the power drugs have over man. In the language of the myth, this corresponds to the fact that Piai'man immediately perceives the children as his apprentices, without the children themselves being aware of the fact.

Unlike the expectations nourished by Western drug users, above all to "obtain" something from the drug, the first stage in the myth's apprenticeship is self-liberation, renunciation, and purification by means of vomiting—a phenomenon physically associated with intoxication, but which also has a psychological meaning. As Eliade has illustrated,[5] vomiting in shamanic rituals is always associated with purification. It is important to note that in the myth vomiting comes *first,* whereas organically speaking it is the result of intoxication. Two other elements in the myth are characteristic of initiation—isolation, especially from the opposite sex , and a direct relationship with nature (for instance, water) and with the vegetative process (the "soul" of the trees).

We now come to the rite of the cords of woven hair. Hair-symbolism is roughly analogous to bird-symbolism in that both hint at man's loftier nature. But hair, which also represents strength (as in the case of Samson), in many cultures represents immortality of the spirit, since it grows out of the head, in most cases remains affixed to it throughout life, and appears to survive after the death of the body. Even in our own culture, renunciation of the world often entails renunciation of one's hair (in religious orders or in the military). There often exists a complex relationship between hair and initiation[6] in primitive cultures.

The fact that in the Arekuna myth the cord of hair enters through the nose and exits through the mouth could serve to emphasize the primacy of intangible or spiritual qualities over material ones, represented here as food. As we have already said, the apprentice shaman not only fasts but also vomits. Otherwise, the vaporous qualities of a drug tend to accentuate its magical-archetypal quality, as will be seen in the "inhalations" of the case study in Chapter Six. The tobacco juice in the myth is fed to the initiates through their noses, in keeping with the fact that tobacco is generally inhaled, but also underscoring the magic forces often associated with the substance—as for example in South America, where it is sometimes self-administered as proof that shamanic powers have been acquired.[7]

Finally, the myth raises a theme we have come across before—the terrible risks entailed by "initiations" into drug use while lacking the necessary preparation, maturity, and moral fortitude. Two of the children go blind and become spirits of the night. Not only do they

5. Eliade, M., *Rites and Symbols of Initiation.* New York: Harper & Row, p. 145; also, Wilson, Bryan, *Magic and the Millenium.* London: Heinemann, 1973, p. 415.

6. See Leach, E., "Magical Hair," in Middleton, J., ed., *Myth and Cosmos.* Austin: University of Texas Press, 1967, pps. 102-103.

7. See Chevalier and Gheerbrant, *op. cit.*, vol. 4, p. 250 (drawn from an article by A. Métraux).

fail to acquire shamanistic powers, but are imprisoned in the unconscious and cannot escape. The remaining children (three, a dynamic
number) grow old with their "lord," serving their shamanic art and
the powers of the drug. Since they have become bald, it appears as
though they have had to sacrifice some part of their individuality in
order to do so.

Drug Addiction and Societal Crisis

We could say that the pathological threshold in drug abuse is
crossed when a repetitive need for a drug appears independently of
any archetypal function. At this point, addiction unequivocally sets in.

Indigenous drugs, such as alcohol in the West, are so familiar that
they rarely arouse the sacred respect conferred the "exotic" drugs we
have already discussed, though not even the archetypal function of
an exotic drug should be taken too literally. A drug's archetypal
function limits its consumption only if sacred respect is translated
into affective ritual accompanying and channeling the use of the drug.
This, in turn, can only happen if the substance is introduced gradually,
not by cynical speculators but rather by those who are in charge of
the sacred and who have greatest respect for sacred traditions. In
reality, new drugs are almost always introduced for commercial reasons and into a culture in crisis. In such a situation, the novelty or
exotic function is no more than bait. It sparks curiosity and makes
initial consumption more frenetic for the unprepared user. The archetypal element activated by the drug is quickly suppressed, and the
user lapses into a repetitive dependence lacking any sacred guarantee
or protection.

The most dramatic example of a cultural descent into drug abuse
is that of the American Indian in the last century. Before examining
the Indian culture's completely secular use of alcohol and sacred use
of peyote, or its inherent need for initiations and esoteric truths, we
should briefly recall how various tendencies in present-day America
evoke and emphasize these aspects of the original American culture.

In the 1960s and 1970s the United States was a culture in crisis,
though certainly not as total a crisis as that faced by the Indians a
century earlier. The widespread popularity of hallucinogens in North
America (such as LSD, peyote and various indigenous mushrooms)

coincided with the self-criticism generated by the war in Vietnam, and in general with a crisis in the political and military leadership of the entire Western world. The use of hallucinogens seems to have taken place, to a large extent, independently of the use of more familiar drugs—a use which already existed and continued to grow. Hallucinogens were openly linked to a genuine widespread interest in "native" cultures. If the military and political supremacy of the United States was no longer absolute, and if all of Western civilization was feeling limited and in need of renewal, then it was natural, culturally speaking, to turn to native cultures which had been militarily defeated but never truly understood. The spread of hallucinogens was closely linked to a rediscovery of Native American culture—a culture founded on initiation, and that initiation in turn founded on the concept of "vision." Thus the psychedelic movement had its prophets (such as Timothy Leary) as well as its gospels (the works of Carlos Castaneda), an endless series of esoteric and initiatory motifs revolving around the wisdom and insight of Native American shamanism.

The movement petered out and after a few years disappeared, but the core of "psychedelic" ideas may have left its mark on the official culture, for instance in the conviction that man cannot be guided by exclusively rationalist criteria, or in the recognition that political and economic intervention satisfies only a small part of real human needs. The irrational element was finally accepted as neither a form of pathology nor an accident on the path of collective psychic development.

The search for "vision," so essential in Amerindian culture, is that archetypal drive which, because of the geographical proximity of the two cultures, led many Americans towards hallucinogens rather than other types of drugs. The "masters" of this psychedelic movement may have been hasty and naively enthusiastic, yet they did attempt to sacralize hallucinogens and to discourage profiteering from their sale. Heroin, on the other hand, was and is a drug sold and circulated with *only* monetary gain in mind. The same applies to the distribution of alcohol among American Indians at the most crucial moment in their history.

Over the last century, Amerindian society has undergone perhaps the worst cultural crisis ever witnessed by Europeans. In the wake of their military defeat, the Indian tribes were generally placed near an Indian Agency on which they began to rely for subsidies and commerce. Nomadism and hunting practically disappeared, along with the pre-established process of individuation that they entailed, and the mythic models they were based on. As we know, this trauma almost destroyed the entire culture and resulted in very high rates of suicide, illnesses, and infant mortality. Above all, it was reflected in epidemic alcoholism. That "legal" European drug reduced the Indian population to ruinous addiction, even though it had always known and used drugs which, from our point of view, were much stronger, though of course being protected from them by the initiatory rites of consumption. It was impossible to re-create around alcohol the esoteric rites which could release the substance's creative aspects, or at least limit its destructive ones. Besides the different effect of alcohol, the impossibility of lessening its impact was assured by at least two cultural factors.

First of all, alcohol was ubiquitous. To the Indian it must have seemed just another aspect of that crass lack of distinction between the sacred and the profane, the hallmark of the European. The Indian lived in a system of taboo, to which contact with objects, and others, as well as the utterance of certain words, was subjected.

Alcohol also came from that European who scorned initiation, who was instead the bearer of death. The American Indian therefore did not associate the substance with hopes of regeneration, but rather with destruction and death. We should not forget that death and regeneration are two obligatory phases in initiation. We can thus see how recourse to alcohol metaphorically reflected an attempt at renewal for those who found themselves in an unbearable situation, but a pessimistic attempt, a kind of surrender, since it responded to the individual and social crisis by opting for a substance which could only supply the first element, death, but not the second, rebirth.

Could this alcoholism represent a collective need for suicide? It is a fact that increased alcoholism was accompanied by a rise in suicides. One could hypothesize an unconscious and desperate attempt, on the part of a society that had lost every shred of autonomy, to be independent in the only way possible—self-destruction.

What we can be sure of is that the sudden introduction of a drug from a foreign culture is extremely risky, though it was more so in the case of the Amerinds than it is in modern America. From the anthropological point of view, this can be explained by a lack of tradition, rites, and wise masters or elders who guide consumers of the drug and protect them from potentially shattering experiences. From the psychological angle, we could say that the entire Native American culture came into contact with its shadow too suddenly, and that this collective shadow (the European world) too quickly came to light.

We know that repression affects the economy of the psyche and cannot be suddenly eliminated; if it is, the result can be explosive disturbances of normal psychic rhythms. Every culture, even the most primitive, has some mechanism to integrate and control the shadow, and to avoid becoming overly distanced from disturbing repressed contents, and thus to have a chance of understanding and gradually exorcizing them. Thus sexuality is not so much censured among "primitives" as it is sacralized and bound up with initiatory rites. The same is true for magic and those forces considered supernatural— they can only be approached through initiation, which unlike sexuality is not available to all.

The power of the shadow can be integrated and controlled through initiatory rites. Initiation consists of sanctifying life's secular and pro-fane elements, and since those elements came from the European world which had abolished all such distinctions, the process of sha-dow-integration was extremely difficult for the native culture. The tremendous difference between the desacralized Euro-American world and the initiation oriented Indian world is best highlighted by the fact that the Indians entrusted their very last attempts at resisting Europeanization to increasingly initiatory and esoteric structures. The Ghost Dance religion and the peyote cult are worth noting in particular.

Wounded Knee is no doubt familiar to all of us, for in 1973 it was the site of the rebirth of an organized Native American nationalism. Wounded Knee was already known as the site of the last battle between Federal and Indian forces which took place in 1890. If history is considered in other than military terms, however, that battle was not the final attempt at Indian resistance, a resistance that was cultural and not military—the founding and the rapid though superficial spread of the Ghost Dance religion, stamped out *militarily* at Wounded Knee, but re-emerging afterwards in various cultural configurations. In this religion, one was initiated into a dance which supposedly would recall the past and the ancestral powers (the ghosts). Their traditions were to reign again, herds of bisons would reappear, and natural disasters and natural forces (not Indian warriors) would wipe the invader off the face of the earth.

A confrontation between a Western culture and a pre-modern symbolic culture can take place as long as it is not on a military or technological plane. The power of the symbol, the sense of sacredness, and initiatory rites are all aspects of pre-modern societies envied by the West, and which individuals are increasingly attempting to relive. The promise made to the initiated Ghost Dancer—that Federal Army weapons would be useless against him—should have been understood metaphorically. The error the dancers fell into was not accepting the truth of the promise on a *symbolic* level, but on a *semiotic* one. They did not recognize the inviolability of the Indian as a symbol *per se*, as an activator of unconscious forces. They translated that "truth" onto another plane, the military plane, with its own signifier and meaning. This mistake hints at an influx of European anti-sacral pragmatism and leads us to suspect that it had already begun to seep into Indian culture.

An initiatory truth is absolute and cannot manifest itself externally unless it is relativized and de-sacralized. In other words, the Ghost Dancers would perhaps really have been invincible had they continued to perceive their invincibility in strictly symbolic and initiatory terms. And yet in context of our attempt to understand the problem, not even their tragic fate appears meaningless, since it points out that every initiatory urge more or less unconsciously activates an archetypal model containing both death and renewal, and that the fragility of the structures activating them can block either initiatory death or renewal.

While regeneration is a purely psychic process, psychic death can be a specific and irreversible organic event. When the initiatory process is not satisfying and complete enough an experience, one can be tempted to persist in it with increasing fury. This insistence can at times lead to an intensification of the material process without necessarily augmenting the psychic one. This can be observed in those drug cases where the archetypal experience remains unreachable and the user pursues it with ever-larger doses. Our hypothesis is that each attempt at initiation which is neither adequately conscious, nor protected by rituals, nor part of a coherent cultural whole, above all activates the "death" element in the archetypal model—both because this is the first and simplest stage, and because, unlike regeneration, it can occur literally as organic death. A need which is not expressed symbolically always tends to become literalized.

The degeneration of the death-and-regeneration process leads to literal death under the adequate cultural conditions. We will deal with the phenomenon later in this chapter. It is useful to mention it here, since it does not seem too far-fetched to hypothesize that any initiatory theme sensitizes the individual to the possibility of death, and that the Ghost Dance itself may have led many of its adherents to a kind of unconscious collective suicide in that tragic Christmas at Wounded Knee. When all the hopes bound to the Ghost Dance religion were broken, a new initiatory cult quickly spread through various tribes in the western part of the United States—this was the peyote cult.

Peyote is a cactus (*Lophophora williamsii*) indigenous to a zone running from Texas to Mexico. Its shoots contain mescaline. Most sources agree that it is a reasonably strong hallucinogen and that it is not addictive. The Conquistadors had encountered rites accompanied by peyote, but these seem to have been minor and isolated cults. Rites linked to peyote broke out in full force only during the last quarter of the last century, right after the definitive Federal military victory. This "explosion" spread both quantitatively (through many varied tribes) and qualitatively (peyotism, wherever it caught on, tended to turn into *the* central ritual). Even recently, peyotism has attracted attention because of its continued spread and growth.[8] In 1951 about

8. Much of the following information on the Ghost Dance and Peyote cults has been drawn from: Wilson, *Magic and the Millenium*, especially chapters nine and thirteen; Eliade, M., *From Primitives to Zen*. New York: Harper and Row, 1977, p. 404ff.; Muhlmann, W.E., *Chiliasmus uns Nativismus*. Berlin: Reimer. Specifically about peyotism: Harner, ed., *op. cit.*; La Barre, W., *The Peyote Cult*. New York: Schocken, 1969 (a classic work on peyotism); Myerhoff, G.B., *Der Peyote Kult*. Munich: Trikont, 1980; Gerber, P., *Die Peyote-Religion*. Zürich: Volkerkundemuseum der Universität Zürich, 1980. For a description of the peyote ceremony from a Jungian standpoint, see Lany, J., "The Peyote Movement, An Introduction," in *Spring 1972*. New York: Spring, 1972.

one fifth of the Navajo population was involved, and about a third in 1964.

The peyote movement is not a cult or a religion in the true sense of the word, nor can we say that peyote has become a cult object (even though it is sometimes equated with Christ). Rather, it is a tool used to find the correct revelatory vision. Its associated creed varies from place to place and is generally syncretistic, with elements of tribal religions as well as Christianity incorporated into it. (John Rave, one of the movement's most important leaders, baptized members "in the name of the Father, the Son, and the Holy Spirit," making a cross on the person's head with peyote juice). It was only in 1955 that the Native American Church of North America was founded. The Church's official founding Act outlines its aims, Christian and moral, but as early as Article Two mentions "the sacrament of peyote." The formation of the Church and its growing acceptance of Christian tradition are generally seen as expediencies adopted as a defense against persecution by the authorities. For our purposes, it is interesting to note that this cult has retained its basic character of a spontaneous initiatory movement and that today it is highly symbolic.

The object of the cult is essentially the vision obtained through peyote—the fact that this is often called the vision of Christ smacks more of justification than anything else. The symbolic nature of this vision is typically Jungian. According to the sociologist Bryan Wilson,

> Only from eating peyote could wisdom be acquired. It could not be described or revealed because it surpassed the power of words to communicate. . . The holy "in-group" following the Peyote Road was essentially a group enjoying a mystic bond. Outsiders could not penetrate its mysteries or understand its meaning. But there are other ethical implications. . . Peyote was said by some to be "tricky" to use. It was, after all, a source of power, and a man must lead a straight life or Peyote would shame him. It was not easy to eat, and there was sometimes a suggestion that to get wisdom men must be prepared to suffer. The meetings thus had some connotation of the ordeal and the proof of worthiness. It could bring bad consequences for the guilty. . . Peyote itself was said to teach men an ethical system, the Peyote Road.[9]

It is no wonder then that in various tribes the word used for peyote

---

9. Wilson, *Magic and the Millenium*, pp. 421-422.

also means "medicine" in general. Finally, we should note here that this cult is symbolic (from the Greek *syn* and *ballein*, "to throw together") insofar as it manages to fuse Christian and animist elements and to reconcile, in the span of only a few years, tribal cultures not only different from one another, but which had kept themselves rigorously distinct.

Second, the peyote movement rose up spontaneously from the ashes of millenarian revolutionary movements such as the Ghost Dance Religion. Many leaders in fact converted from one cult to the other. Peyotism, however, seemed to have a good chance of lasting since it didn't prophesy the disappearance of the invader but actually accepted part of his culture, for example, elements of Christianity. It was no longer a desperate sort of defence, but now a successful one guaranteeing the cohesion of the group around a culture no longer a culture of the past, nor simply an assimilation of European culture. The seeds of this new message were sown on personal and interior ground. The awareness of an unusually cruel and virtually irreparable human situation led many to an extreme withdrawal from the world. The only real collective aspect in all of this was the strong cohesion of the community around the rite. In Bryan Wilson's classification, the movement is termed *introversionist*. The answer to evil proposed by the Ghost Dance Religion is termed *revolutionist*.

These historical and sociological distinctions are worth pointing out because the analogy between the fate of the Ghost Dance movement and that of today's protest movements is striking. The majority of these protest movements dissolve as soon as the aim of reaching political power (revolution) is lost. Esoteric groups (introversion) including terroristic groups (which obviously have an initiatory aspect to them) and more and more noticeable groups of drug users, spring up in parallel and often with direct ties to the protest movements. If these groups—which are apparently dissimilar—are born out of one another, then they must have something in common, such as for example the eschatological moment which is experienced, more or less consciously, by both revolutionary and esoteric groups.

Third, the peyote movement was initiatory in every respect. We know that initiation can be divided into two main groupings: collective initiation (puberty rites provided for all) and individual initiation (the admission of a chosen few to secret societies or shamanism). The Great Plains Indians generally considered the search for vision as obligatory in puberty as well as at other moments in life, and peyote was the instrument which encouraged these rites. In those tribes with strong shamanic institutions (for instance the Mescaleros), peyote became for the most part a shamanic tool. In time, a fragmentary situation came about: in theory everyone could be admitted to the rite, but in practice, as we have seen, not everyone was worthy of it. As far as the Indian nation as a whole is concerned, initiation has become, at least potentially, part of a common heritage. Though there no longer exists a purely Indian culture independent of European culture, initiation in peyotism is, as a rule, reserved only for Indians.

The cult of peyotism seeks to confirm membership in the Native American heritage, and to recoup lost dignity by endowing the group with a greater transcendent value. Here we find yet another striking analogy with those marginal groups of "outsiders" in our own society.

Fourth, the peyote movement drastically condemns the use of alcohol. Otherwise, the ethical principles of peyotism are simple and moralistic. They include brotherhood, the family, work, the condemnation of lies and of sexual promiscuity. John Raven, whom we have already mentioned, was an ex-alcoholic converted to peyotism.

On one hand, this is a specifically Indian phenomenon, part of an attempt to retrieve a sense of national identity and to renew ties with traditions different from those of the invader. On the other hand, however, it confirms the fact that there is a certain amount of fanaticism and intolerance potentially present in initiatory groups (and therefore in those who use drugs in general) and among converts (we might call them initiates who have to make up for lost time, or prosletyzing initiates such as St. Paul, with his frenetic activism, or many members of Alcoholics Anonymous). In any event, a person who chooses a particular drug develops a sense of mistrust for other substances.

Fifth, let us finally take a look at how the peyote ceremony is actually carried out. The rite takes place at night; symbolically this confirms that what is being sought is contact with the unconscious, and that the cult's original intent was to strengthen the visions which had up until then been achieved through simple dreams, which comprise a central religious experience for Indian life.

There are prayers and songs throughout the ceremony. As is the case with many secret societies, initially only men were admitted (even though the presiding diety was often feminine; even though a Kiowa myth tells of how peyote was given to men by a woman; and even though the participants gathered round a mound of earth shaped like the moon, a feminine symbol in many cultures). During the night, a drum is beaten, water is drunk and the participants vomit, a practice considered positive since it is purifying.

On the whole, we can evaluate peyotism as a collective movement and as an individual experience which aims at renewing both the psyche of the individual and of the group with the help of new forces or elements revived through visions obtained from the drug. From the psychological point of view, it is not easy to evaluate to what extent peyotism, as opposed to the Ghost Dance, is a kind of creative sublimation or resigned rationalization. One thing, however, is certain—between the two there is a relationship of mutual substitution. Going back for a moment to the three-fold division we have proposed of drug addiction, we could say that these movements can replace each other as far as the expression of the third, archetypal element is concerned. As we have seen, alcohol can replace peyote as far as the first two elements are concerned, but not the third, because of the ritual and symbolic poverty of alcohol.

The most significant myth of peyotism refers to the cult's renewal function. Again, the citation is drawn from Bryan Wilson:

> . . . an Indian girl, who had gone to the hills to bewail the absence and presumed death of her brothers, lost her way and, worn out with grief, lay down to sleep. In her dreams the peyote spirit visited her and promised that her brothers should be found, and that where her head rested she would find that which would restore them to her. The spirit gave further instructions and vanished. Next day, she dug up the peyote which she found where her head had rested, and returned to her camp with the plant and the story of her vision. Under her direction the sacred tipi was set up with its crescent mound. Songs were sung, prayers said, and peyote was eaten, and in their visions the old men

saw where the warriors were wandering. The warriors were recovered from the enemy country, and since then "peyote is eaten by the Indians with song and prayer that they may see visions and know inspiration, and the young girl who first gave it is venerated as the Peyote woman."[10]

What the myth thus speaks of is a psychic situation in which both wisdom and tradition (the elders) are present, as well as feeling and creativity (the young girl). What is missing is willful action, or the dynamic qualities of the ego (the warriors). These forces can be rediscovered and renewed through the visions induced by peyote, for this substance acts as an intermediary between conscious elements and the elements which have been lost or have become unconscious. It plays the same role as the analyst in our culture and on the individual plane.

With all of its rites, peyotism represents a turning point from a traditional use of drugs to a more modern one. In context of the traditional Indian culture, the vision, with its collective meaning, is of central importance. The drug itself is not absolutely necessary. This transition opens the way to the modern use of drugs, where the vision, if indeed sought at all, loses its importance, its sacredness, and its collective significance.

The Assassins

In order to really understand the relationship between the psyche and the two factors of drugs and initiation, as well as the relationship between the two factors—drugs and initiation—it is important to exercise (and to stimulate) our archetypal imagination. Unfortunately the collective values and rational conscious categories of our culture are of little help. It is a far from easy task to rid our understanding of prejudices.

Grasping an archetypal fantasy entails receiving a deep impression which somehow manages to filter through our categorical prejudiced way of thinking, then immediately afterwards using those same categories in order to express what has been imprinted by the archetype. Whenever we want to express ourselves, we do so by bringing the center of our consciousness in line with the culture in which we live.

10. Wilson, *Magic and the Millenium*, pp. 420-421.

It is a great satisfaction for us when we can let our consciousness wander about lazily for a moment, for then, when hearing of an actual or mythical event in primitive peoples, we can allow it to "impress" us to the point of recognizing in ourselves an analagous archetypal fantasy—something like closing one's eyes while listening to primitive music and letting oneself be carried away by it, which could also be a way of understanding the ceremony in which that music was played. The comparison is useful because we realize that serving up historical and ethnological information out of context, as a side dish to a psychological main course, can seem harsh and brutal. We analysts are often accused of rummaging through the lives of primitives in search of elements that can be of use to us, without however duly deepening our knowledge of the whole context. But if the point of all this is to listen to a piece of music or a song, a hunting song for example, with our eyes closed, to see if the feeling of being a hunter or the urge to dance is sparked off within us, then we can say that our limited vision is useful; for we are not anthropologists out to understand as deeply as possible the society of bison hunters, for example, but rather psychologists out to discover whether in those elements which inspired various peoples to the hunt there might not be elements in common with ourselves. All we can say is that our hope is to feel the ancient archaic hunter down inside ourselves by listening to that piece of music or that song.

As far as psychology is concerned, the criteria of scientific objectivity cannot unfortunately be upheld, for the psyche is both the object under observation and the subject which observes. The most reasonable way to face up to the contradiction is simply to accept it. This is why the most important part of an analyst's training is his own personal analysis. With this in mind, we apologize for any violence we may have done to material from non-European cultures, and shall continue along the path of this study. We should like to propose examining a legend which, besides dealing mainly with the use of drugs, also tells of the formation of an esoteric sect. Admittance to this sect, the secret society of Alamut, was extremely difficult and was subject to a most amazing initiatory ritual.

It is impossible to determine from available information to what extent the central historical element has been distorted, or to know how many of these possible alterations are the work of Oriental sources and how many of European ones. Though difficult to place in a historical context, the story is of interest to us both because of its psychological significance and because we feel that it speaks to our archetypal imagination.

Of the many accounts of the Alamut available, the most famous is by Marco Polo. The story, which we shall summarize here in our own words, runs like this:

> A powerful man known as "the old man of the mountain" had the most beautiful gardens one could imagine. There were streams that flowed with milk, honey and wine, and beautiful young maidens danced and sang in the meadows. But every now and then the old man gave a mysterious drink to a young boy. The young boy would lose his senses and be carried into the garden. He would awaken and be convinced that he had ended up in paradise. From time to time the old man would have someone from his court drink the liquid again, and this time he would have him taken into the palace. Upon awakening, the young man would be ordered to kill someone. The killer was assured that if he succeeded he would be taken back to the garden-paradise of the old man. If he was killed in the attempt, he would obtain more or less the same results, according to the Koran. Needless to say, the executions were carried out most efficiently, and for a long time everyone in the region subjected themselves to "the old man" and paid tribute to him.

Those who belonged to the sect were called Hāshshāshin, a term which in Arabic means "hashish people" and is transliterated as "Assassins." The terror they spread came to an end when they were wiped out by the Tartars in the middle of the thirteenth century.

These stories have always had a powerful effect on the European imagination, but not until the beginning of the nineteenth century did they become the object of serious study. The French orientalist deSacy identified the Hāshshāshin as the extremist Shi'ite Ismailite sect, which in the years following 1000 AD fought against both the Islamic orthodoxy of the Caliphate and the Crusaders, spreading bloodshed through Persia and Syria. The sect was made up of a small number of members and therefore never took to the battlefield as such, but rather perfected a system of political assassination which gradually made it invincible. The term "assassin" is said to derive from this. The Arab term, however, comes from the rite of eating hashish so as not to be afraid of one's own death or upset by the death of others.

It should be pointed out that various stories, including those reconstructed by expert orientalists, are vague as to the real nature of the drug, calling it anything from hashish to opium. The narrators of the stories do not seem to be particularly interested in knowing more about the drug, but rather seem to have an unconscious propensity for vagueness, almost as if they wanted to preserve that esoteric and mysterious quality which our archetypal imagination associates with drug initiation.

It is not a proven fact that hashish was used ritually before killings by Assassins, although adherents of the theory have made it into tradition in Islamic culture—some even believe that the practice was revived and used against the French in Algeria.

More recent studies have shed some light on the mysteries of the sect. The Assassins was an extremely select elite devoted to its cause. The group was exclusively male (*Männerbund*, like many secret societies) with intense mystical commitment and fanatical conviction of truth. It seems significant that the collective European imagination has cast the Alamut, above and beyond the complex historical truth, as the prototypical criminal organization, a fact reflected unequivocally in our language. With the exception of German, the main European languages have adopted the term "assassin" to indicate one who premeditatively murders another, even though these languages already had words to express this idea.

Absolute negative projection is the simplest and most drastic way of confronting something upsetting and yet fascinating and unknowable at the same time. Since the condemnation of evil is necessary, it creates a system allowing one to take an interest in the mysterious element, yet allowing simplicity of the judgement to overcome the uneasiness and the ambivalence of that interest. These are things we always see—one need only think of the ease with which we express all kinds of negative judgements about rich or powerful, famous people, even though we don't know them at all. It is all too easy to verify that a potential danger of falling into the same sort of prejudices exists when we express judgements about groups of drug users or terrorists. Both of these groups are very close—much closer than the average man—to death. Often they are the very ones who administer it (the first group to themselves, the second group to others). By behaving as they do, they assume a power yet ignore a taboo in a way which causes scandal and maybe gives rise to a certain amount of secret envy as well.

Too little attention is generally paid to the fact that our unconscious envy, which we then deny with an overly simplified type of negative projection, is not only envy of the chance to take drugs or to shoot at someone, but it is also envy of the initiate, of he or she who has contact with another dimension, someone to whom a truth has been revealed, or who has enjoyed an experience denied the average man. This hypothesis helps us to understand better why the myth of Alamut in Western eyes (*Alamut*, by the way, means "eagle's nest," and this is significant since metaphors of flight and height are often found in connection with initiation or drugs) was entirely steeped in terrorism and drugs. Due to the extremely strict esoterism of the group on the one hand, and its total annihilation by the Tartars on the other, the only people who spoke about the sect for centuries were unfortunately not its supporters, but rather its enemies. These enemies spoke only about the perverse aspects of the sect, and so it is hard to distinguish reality from moralistic fantasies, or from the shadow projections of the speaker. From what we can gather from recent studies and investigations, the structure of the sect consisted of one of the most rigid religious initiations ever known, while drugs and terrorism were ancillary. And yet popular legends have to be expressed in terms of available concepts, and since initiation had all but disappeared in the West, the imagination of the European dwelt on the tip of the iceberg, the most obvious phenomena capable of sparking intense curiosity: drugs and terrorism. The same thing happens today. We are immediately interested in the material activities of those groups about which we know too little, but we don't realize that what has really roused our curiosity is the initiatory atmosphere of the group.

There are many elements of the Alamut legend which strike us as being significant and which, aside from the particular cultural situation in which they arose, have some fairy-tale qualities about them. They are, in short, decidedly archetypal. These elements include the old man who is a master, but a master of misdeeds; the strict, unnatural separation of the initiate from the outside world; the absence of independent will in the initiates, in terms of both awareness and morals; and a lack of concrete information on the sect's rituals of purification and renunciation, or for that matter, on any of its rituals. It seems that the Alamut's first initiatory phase, the phase of separation and death, is cut off and projected onto whoever is not a member of the sect. Thus the death-experience is reserved for the enemy.

We are struck by the Alamut's either proud or simplistic or absolutist use of drugs, which springs from a simplistic or absolutist ideology. The killing of an external enemy could be an allegorical unconscious representation of the gradual dissolution of the initiate's previous identity (the sect sprang from and fought against the more orthodox Islamic world), along with that part of his personality not yet incorporated into the circle of drug users. The "other" dies, not one's own ego. The process of Alamut initiation, with its obedience to a perverse master and its apparent tendency toward restricting rather than enriching interior experience, could fall into the classification which, in Chapter Two, we termed *negative initiation.*

The entire legend, however, has the flavor of a warning, especially given the old man's pride, and the rise then sudden and utter destruction of the sect—almost as if the story were a parable about the downfall of pride, about the reckless and evil use of drugs. The story could also be interpreted as a warning against undergoing initiation while lacking humility of heart and mind, or about the degeneration that sets in when a sect becomes overly proud of its esoteric power. Since most stories about the sect emphasize its secrecy rather than its use of drugs, it seems that the real danger is embodied in the latter instead of in the former.

The preponderance of negative elements in stories about the Alamut should make us wary, however, especially if we imagine that the story corresponds to historical reality. Aside from the vagueness of tales about the sect circulating in Medieval Europe, scholars have until very recently had to rely on tales recorded by the sect's adversaries—who, after wiping out the sect itself, also destroyed its writings. The possibility thus remains that initiation into the sect represented access to a world of faith and significant esoteric wisdom. Our suspicions are aroused by the way both Europe and the Middle East disseminated only negative information on the sect, especially by using its name to designate the very worst of crimes. We have no real evidence—though this visceral aversion does constitute some proof—but we can assert that the fate of the Alamut legend corresponds with a collective tendency, especially in terms of initiation, to strengthen central power structures and to eliminate ancillary ones. What this tendency sought to accomplish was to encourage collective values to adopt an acritical condemnation of those initiatory groups with the greatest autonomy—one need only think of the violent crusades against the Templars and the Albigensians conducted by the Church.

Naturally, this moralism struck most virulently against those groups that had established a more or less absolute autonomy—achieved through the development of an independent "vision" and ideology, separation from the surrounding world, both functional and esoteric, and perhaps also the creation of a special mystic atmosphere through mind-altering experiences (flagellation, drugs, and so on). The schematic nature of this moralistic condemnation reveals that the culture dominant in the Middle Ages was already pressing for the elimination of esoterism and genuine initiatory structures. This has continued through to our own days (perhaps even more intensely, given the dominant collective imperative of rationalism), and the only path remaining open to the expression of these two phenomena is a negative one.

CHAPTER 5

DEATH AND REBIRTH,
AND THE DEATH OF REBIRTH

The Death of the Ego

From the beginning of this study we have stressed that death and regeneration are the key to every initiatory process.[1] At the risk of sounding repetitive, let us quickly run through the main points of this idea once again.

In primitive societies, the relationship between initiation and death is so close that many initiatory procedures are analagous to death-rites.[2] The relationship is also mutual: not only does initiation lead to a spiritual death, but material death itself is interpreted in an initiatory sense, as part of a process which necessarily leads to rebirth.[3]

1. *The Enciclopedia delle Religioni* (6 vols. Firenze: Vallecchi editore, 1970) criticizes the wide and general way in which the concept of initiation is used today; yet it recognizes that in this concept there is an element which unites eight categories of events otherwise classified separately. It should be noted that already in the work by van Gennep (who is considered a pioneer in this area, even though he dealt with rites of passage and not initiation) a similar outline is followed: *separation, marge, agrégation,* where *separation* stands for psychological death to one's previous environment and status, and *marge* stands for an intermediate state between it and the regenerative one of *agrégation.*
2. See the *Enciclopedia delle Religioni,* Vol. 3, p. 1131.
3. See, for example, the chapter on death in Eliade's *Occultism ,Witchcraft and Cultural Fashions.* Chicago: University of Chicago Press, 1976.

These remarks on the duality of death-initiation, seemingly the province of anthropology, have great value when applied to our own society. We have already hypothesized a latent need for initiation in our modern society, and this leads us to suspect that the turning to drugs *en masse,* along with the corollary establishment of esoteric groups, is a disorderly and desperate expression of this need. Our society lacks initiation rituals, but is also so lacking in death rituals that death has often been perceived as the great repressed theme of our century, comparable to the sex taboo of the last century. In light of what has been said so far, it would be difficult to see this as only a coincidence. Death and initiation are archetypally related terms. Not only have death and initiation both been repressed, but they belong to the same area of repression. It is in the world of drugs that the theme of death is continually activated.

We often come across people who say that they have turned to drugs with the desire of dying little by little. Even when the physical death of the individual is not an issue, psychic death is still constellated. One often turns to drugs because of the insignificance, senselessness and flatness of one's present life, a dead and senseless thing fueled by solely reflex action.

When one's family values, affections and ideals are all dead, then one searches for a life experience worthy of that name, even if it is a question of a purely subjective experience shared by a restricted few. One feels a kind of progressive psychic death as the effects of the substance wear off (generally speaking though, this experience is different depending on whether the substance in question is heroin, alcohol, or substances derived from cannabinoids, etc.). As far as heavy drugs are concerned, the user typically experiences a sensation of death during periods of abstinence, and this can be felt with great physical intensity—which probably contributes to the exaggerated importance granted physical addiction, as we have already mentioned.

One thus cannot help but notice that a link exists between turning to drugs and the unconscious theme of death-and-renewal. The battle of life against death is, to be sure, the matrix of every meaningful action we perform, but this matrix is especially evident in the case of the drug addict.[4] The taking of drugs is not part of the life-death opposition in some vague and general sense. With every dose, one can literally (and not just metaphorically) eliminate life, and provided that one does not go too far, make it begin all over again. Every dose is more or less unconsciously linked with the expectation of death-rebirth, and creates it *de facto*. This expectation is, as we know, an ambivalent one, where the death-element can easily prevail not only physically, but also in terms of deeper psychic experience. But this expectation is at the same time, in its pure form, an attempt to create a form of self-initiation.

This attempt, besides being for the most part unconscious, is carried out today in a historical and cultural situation which is anything but favorable, inevitably overlooking the importance of paradigmatic mythologies and of masters who could offer some kind of orientation within the experience. The initiatory attempt is not aware of the distinction between the sacred and the profane nor the respect which has, from ancient times, been due to the sacred. It likewise ignores the preparatory or purificatory sacrifices which accompany and limit the use of drugs, as is the case in primitive societies. The attempt is thus bound to fail, not so much because of the inadequacy and danger of its means, but because of the circumstances and the ways in which this attempt manifests itself.

Despite all attempts made to ritualize the use of drugs, there are two errors which are committed in turning to these substances—naiveté and shortsightedness. Not only are the toxicological obstacles insufficiently taken into account, but the corresponding cultural and psychological obstacles are underestimated. The body reacts by showing signs of poisoning, and, since it is not capable of integrating the experience, so does the psyche.

Let us go a step beyond cultural naiveté and try to look at this lack of success from the archetypal point of view. Does the model of initiation, the impulse to experience death and rebirth, carry out its

4. This holds true not only for the present-day use of drugs. For example, a German treatise on intoxication dating from 1830 (F.F. von Baader, *Ueber den Begriff der Ekstasis als Metastasis*) affirms that it is not the physical danger but the experience of the fear of death which is behind the bourgeois taoos against intoxication. See Mattenklott, G., *Der Übersinnliche Lieb*, Hamburg: Reibek, 1982, pp. 225-226.

function? To a certain extent we have to admit that it is activated and that both sides of the model of initiation are constellated. On the other hand, the dynamic of the archetype always sets off an exchange between two opposite poles and can develop in an ambivalent way.[5] An attempt at initiation can end up by paradoxically affirming death rather than rebirth.

To be exact, we should point out that when taking a drug, there occurs an early phase which could be called the death phase. This consists in a relief from the tensions and worries of the moment, something we might even call the death of contingency. The great goals and strong emotions are not lost (they are actually felt in an exalted way), but what do vanish are the worries we were oppressed by until just a moment before. We know, for example, that soldiers at times turn to alcohol just before an attack (this is true in modern times, but even Homer mentions the same thing); and as we have already seen when examining the Alamut legend, the Assassins are said to have been given that name because they took hashish as a preparatory ritual before their murderous expeditions.

These things could be summarily explained with the assertion that alcohol and hashish provide a certain courage in the face of death. But with such an explanation we risk saying nothing. Psychologically, it is a tautology. From this point of view we could ask what courage is. Is it the negation of death, or a casual relationship with it? Perhaps the help that comes from alcohol and hashish does not consist of distancing the idea of death, but to the contrary, of a moment of untraumatic familiarity with it, manifested in a sensation of distance from, or irrelevance of, every contingent problem. Not by chance, in traditional societies these were goals sought after in preparation for death.

In analytic terms, we can thus say that in the moments following the taking of a drug one experiences a more or less intense ego-death, and a distancing of that consciousness, rationality, and lucidity

5. Even everyday pop psychology and traditional lore affirm that love contains a charge of potential hate and vice versa. But let us take some more specific archetypal themes. For example, the battle of the hero against darkness or against the primeval chaos of unconsciousness, which we have already referred to, can give birth to awareness and to a solid ego but it can also, out of recklessness, go too far and build up a fragile ego which will once again be swallowed up by the unconscious (as happens in a psychosis) thus awarding a victory to the opposing pole.

to which we are bound by the inevitable imperative of European culture. This observation can help us understand certain facts. The use of drugs is considered a crime, especially in the West, because it above all is an attack against the specificity of Western psychology. The fact that drug addiction explodes with particular violence in societies involved in overly hasty modernization can also be seen as an unconscious and desperate attempt on the part of many people to offset the psychic onesidedness which this process causes. It becomes easier for us to understand how in the West drugs are often linked, perhaps unconsciously, with other forms of rejecting the dominant culture.

It is highly improbable that the brief and relative experience of "ego-death" consequent to the taking a drug (a feeling of "ego-lightness") corresponds to the necessity of death in the initiatory archetype, or that it can satisfy this need. This death is not consciously accepted, nor is it experienced as death, but rather as a loosening of excessive tension. When the ego is de-activated, the unconscious is simultaneously activated, overtly when the drug is a hallucinogen, and less overtly when other substances are used.

In general, it seems that in the first minutes following the taking of a drug, the psyche as a whole does not experience a feeling of death, but of alteration. The moment in which the death-experience manifests itself most violently generally occurs afterwards, as the effects of the drug wear off. If we consider drug addiction as an unconscious attempt at self-initiation, then what strikes us the most is that it is an initiation which has been inverted—rebirth as the initial experience, death as the final one.

Negative Initiation

At this point we must ask ourselves whether the two types of initiation discussed so far, "inverted" and "negative," are substantially identical in their archetypal manifestations. It would seem so. In both cases what we are dealing with is a downward initiation, an initiation towards a lower form of life, or towards non-life, or darkness—an initiation in keeping with our times. As Jung said, the old gods, suppressed rather than eliminated, have become diseases and psychic infections. Nietzsche's "death of God" shrugged off positive religion, especially Christianity. But the death-bearing divinities have been strengthened, as is apparent not so much from neo-satanic cults as from the indirect yet shocking potential destructiveness of ideologies. We might even hazard to say that the death of God fosters the god of death. In this view, ritual, though not actually eliminated, functions only in a shadowy way, and initiation reappears as homage to metaphoric gods of the underworld.

Those drug addicts who have a greater sense of awareness in general openly admit to their own self-destructiveness. They say that they prefer to approach death little by little, gradually letting themselves go in that direction while leaving the decision as to the exact moment of death to chance. Even if we interpret this as the need to pass on to a radically new situation, death is still not sought and openly confronted—as it once was by the initiate, who was required to both face an experience of psychic death and to overcome perilous trials. The death of the drug addict is, for the most part, something faced passively.

Those who are most conscious of their self-destructiveness and who are most openly contaminated by the archetype of the negative hero appear to be characters who have chosen a radical and dramatic role, but who hesitate in translating its consequences into action. What is missing is the hero's energy and will power, along with his ability to assume responsibility for his own destiny. Consciousness feels the strength of the archetypal model, but cannot adhere to it completely; everywhere we look we see drugs that bring death, but not renewal. Death is postponed and relegated to the end of a process which, insofar as it is archetypal, tends to unfold autonomously once established, since it does not follow conscious choice as much as it does the unconscious urges of a pre-established model. Even the most aware of drug addicts lives in a kind of tormenting ambivalence, in a daily compromise between the need for radical and definitive change and the little escape route of his daily habit.

The profanity of cultural circumstances does not allow the need for renewal to develop in a calm and solemn process, endowed with that respect for the sacred which the psyche needs in order for the internal experience to be worth something. The consumerism instilled into every member of our society not only encourages him to hasten his experimentation with drugs and their effects, but also represents itself as a sort of profane pseudo-ritual. This pseudo-ritual, in that degenerated form we call obsessive, allows an outlet for the archaic need for ritual now suppressed by our society.

The drug user has thus reversed the model—rebirth comes in the first moments of euphoria, then comes death. Renunciation is denied as a necessary psychological phase, but later manifests itself as biological deprivation, when the substance taken ceases to have an effect on the body of the user. It can also be hypothesized that renunciation imposes itself as a psychological element of the archetype that cannot be eliminated, as a return—unconsciously desired by the user—of repressed materials.

This whole psychological process could also be described by Melanie Klein's concept of "position" instead of the archetypal model, since the concept corresponds in many ways to the idea of archetype.[6] According to Klein, the various possible experiences of depression in the life of an individual are patterned on a model experienced as a necessary moment in early infancy. This moment comes when the child perceives the mother in her entirety; she is no longer, for example, only the good object (linked to the nourishing function of the breast), but an indivisible complex entity who is also perceived as being bad, and who arouses the child's aggression with her imposition of limits and restrictions. ". . . (T)he child comes to know its mother as a whole person and becomes identified with her as a whole, real, and loved person. It is then that the depressive position . . . comes to the fore."[7]

This early experience comprises the basis for later experiences of depression (and analogously, for paranoid and maniacal experiences):

> If the infant at this period of life fails to establish its loved object within—if the introjection of the 'good' object miscarries—then

6. Melanie Klein explains that in her studies of early infancy she moved from the concept of phase to that of position because the very same mechanisms—paranoid, manic and depressive— which act upon the small child remain potentially active all through life. Thus from the study of those phases one can obtain a better understanding of, for example, manic-depressive states in adults. See Klein, Melanie, "A Contribution to the Psychogenesis of Manic-Depressive States," in *Love, Guilt and Reparation*. New York: Delacorte, 1977.

7. Klein, p. 286.

the situation of the 'loss of the loved object' arises already as it is found in the adult melancholic.[8]

The working through and the overcoming of the suffering resultant from the loss of the "good" object, and from feelings of guilt for having been aggressive towards it, are linked to the Kleinian concept of reparation:

> The reparation-tendencies which play an all-important part in the normal process of overcoming the infantile depressive position are set going by different methods, of which I shall just mention two fundamental ones: the manic and the obsessive defences and mechanisms.[9]

We cannot help noticing that the processes described by Klein comprise a model which, in a pathological manifestation, tends to be repeated in drug addiction. Just as we have seen in the case of the depressive position, in cases of drug use feelings of guilt play a great role, and the drug user often dreams up naive and decisive forms of reparation. The maniacal and obsessive tone of repeated, continued, and frenetic recourse to drugs is the same tone of modern consumerism in general, whose most obviously unhealthy aspect is drug addiction.

The use of drugs always brings about an attempt at introjecting the neither unfailingly stable nor permanent "good object," and therefore does not succeed by the time the "good effect" (or ecstatic effect) of the drug wears off in the body of the user.

But given that the progression (or the regression to a schizoparanoid situation) is to a large extent entrusted to the processes of reparation, one could presume that the drug addict is unconsciously motivated by both the need to feel and work through reparation and a form of self-absolution from guilt through self-sacrifice. We would be justified in this presumption even if we often consider this reparative process as being animated by a pure desire of regressing to ecstatic or "oceanic" conditions corresponding to the situation that existed before the establishment of a stable ego. In Klein's opinion, reparation and guilt feelings are not pathological experiences or deviations from the natural process of growth, but necessary phases in the development of the ego and in the acquisition of the normal

8. *Ibid.,* p. 287.
9. *Ibid.,* p. 288.

ability to love. The narcissism and the fragility of the drug addict show that he has not passed through those phases. We can presume that he unconsciously searches for experiences of loss in an attempt to fill this void.

We note that the Kleinian point of view offers a view of individual development outlined according to phases and passages. This progression is seen in terms of natural development as far as early infancy is concerned. But the hypothesis of its continued unconscious existence (in the form of positions which can be reactivated) allows us to see it as a potential model which shows up on later moments of life, and as a natural model constituting the substratum of cultural phenomena, such as initiation, in which the passage to new phases is predicated on the experience of both mourning and of loss (loss of previous identity in place of the "loss of the object of love" in early infantile identification). The natural Kleinian model therefore has a basic structure which is consonant both with the fundamental processes of initiation and with the unconscious need underlying drug use. The fact that in practice drugs constellate the theme of initiation but invert it is even more enlightening if we observe the user not only during a normal period of use, but over a long period of time, including attempts to get off the drug. In these cases, abstinence is tolerated with great efforts in an attempt at renewal or "turning over a new leaf." But after the experience of vitality felt during use, abstinence often brings about a death-experience, and here too the process is inverted, at least as far as is most easily observable aspects are concerned.

There is yet another point of view which can support the line of reasoning we have followed thus far: the clinical picture of drug addiction usually employed by authors combining Freudian and traditional psychopathological approaches. A close look at this literature[10] reveals something that the reader has probably already noticed— the close affinity between the habitual cycle of drug (or alcohol) consumption and the manic-depressive syndrome. We won't go into the question of which comes first, *i.e.* if drug use brings about this syndrome or if the people who turn to drugs are individuals who are

10. Rosenfeld offers a rather exhaustive summary of the literature on this question. See Rosenfeld, H., *Psychotic States*, London: Hogarth Press, 1965.

already potentially manic-depressive. For the time being it is the close link between these two phenomena that interests us.

Manic behavior is characterized by an excessive and fragile, or empty, vitality, and by a feeling of having to constantly undertake new experiences at the expense of those already begun. The manic individual is like someone who has just been born and is greedy for life. In depression, on the other hand, an atmosphere of sadness and death surrounds his every experience. The vitality and energy of the ego could be said to be dead or bound up in endless mourning. Some writers point out that this kind of cycle is characteristic of the drug addict, both in his general on-going life (manic-depressive cycles last, for the most part, at least some months) and within the short cycles of recourse to or consumption of the drug (drunkenness with a feeling of euphoria, followed by feeling "down" in the hours and days that follow).

The vicious circle the drug addict is caught in is what pushes him towards greater and greater doses in the useless search for a condition in which the death experience can be avoided. The paradoxical result, however, is that this can lead to actual physical death. The greater the dose, the more anguished and "deadly" the subsequent state of deprivation and all the more difficult for the addict to accept deprivation as a necessary phase, even if it is seen as a preparatory moment for the next time he takes the drug. The phase of deprivation is suppressed, switched off, overcome, or skipped if at all possible. The user tries to keep death from existing, at least for the moment, then later on whatever happens, happens. In this manic-depressive landscape of peaks and valleys, the drug addict tries to survive like an acrobat, jumping from peak to peak. At times he can't even help being proud of his courage, since he knows he is an acrobat without a safety net.

The drug addict expresses, in an extreme and dangerous form, an attitude which does not belong to him alone but to all of society. There is, in fact, a close analogy between addiction and consumeristic behavior, a type of behavior which can never stop but keeps running after itself, which does not accept downhill trends or giving up what it has, nor tolerates any decrease in goods or services. The drug user who rejects the dominant values of his society is at times aware of his consumerist stamp, and this often leads him to hate himself even more. Compared with more traditional cultures, ours is an abnormal manic formation which leans so far towards the future that it can only keep from falling by running ever faster and more frenetically.

No other culture before ours has believed in uninterrupted and linear forward development. Not only was this technically impossible in the past, but it was also condemned by value systems which somehow included the search for a sense of measure and of self-limitation. On the contrary, the "constant-growth" value system affirmed in the West over the past few decades envisions an ever-growing accumulation of goods and material progress, tenaciously refusing to accept that sadness and renunciation can have a meaning, or to reflect on the mortality of both man and things. We can see, within society itself, the mythologization of its own self-contempt in the spreading of prophesized Great Crises, Great Collapses, and Great Nemeses: the same self-contempt is apparent in society's masochistic taste for catastrophic spectacles—which take some real life episode as their starting point, such as the sinking of the Titanic, but then go on to weave a sort of fairy tale in which man's pride in technology is punished by the forces of nature. It is important for us not to miss the analogy between cultural consumerism, the drug addict's need for bigger and bigger doses, and the fragile and repressive vitalism of the manic. The basic model, expressed at various levels, is the same. The archetypal point of view allows us to embrace clinical observations (the manic-depressive cycle) along with sociological reflections (consumeristic behavior) on drug addiction, not contradicting them but seeking to integrate them into our perspective, and to understand the unconscious tendencies underlying drug use.

The extension of the model onto various planes, the cultural in this chapter, the individual in the next, allows us to broaden the scope of this study to include not only a phenomenological and pathological analysis of drug addiction, but also some consideration on the underlying sense of the problem, on the basic psychic need—not only destructive—at the root of the problem. Examining drug use through the initiatory model allows us to compare this behavior with more general cultural behaviors, and thus verify the universality of the phenomenon, while simultaneously pointing out the specific characteristics of Western culture which do now allow a return to more archaic (and sacralized) conditions. There is much room for discussion as to how this one-sidedness can be remedied, but the ancient rituals are excluded *a priori*.

We should like to add one more consideration concerning the general value of our argument It is relatively easy to assert that the typical drug addict, the user of heavy drugs, has an unconscious need for death—the argument is generally accepted and well-proven. It is also relatively easy to accept both our initiatory model and the hypothesis that the drug user's error consists in haste typical of consumerism, which leads him to invert the initiatory model. Thus the model begins with renewal and ends with the death experience.

Yet what we are suggesting is an archetypal *model* which can help us understand an extreme and specific phenomenon (drug addiction) from the starting point of the hypothesis of a natural need, a universal need which is anything but morbid (i.e. initiation or, more generally, rebirth). Let us apply this model to a more common and accessible example.

Under certain circumstances, many people let themselves go and take too large a dose of that legal drug called "alcohol." This can happen when we find ourselves in "the right atmosphere" which sweeps us, like a wave, into a new and pleasant dimension. The next morning we wake up with a feeling of emptiness and malaise, both physical and psychological. Let us pause for a moment and consider this unpleasant re-awakening, the hangover. In this instance many people feel a sense of guilt, especially if the same thing has already happened at frequent intervals. (In these cases there is already a compelling element which, whether we like it or not, manifests itself as drug addiction). The various rational evaluations one attempts to make when hung over (e.g. "Why did I let myself do that" or "The fun isn't worth the hangover, I should know better by now") are somewhat pathetic. The whole process is an unconcscious rite foreign to the ego's rationality. Even this apparent rational evaluation is, in reality, an obligatory and pre-constituted ritual—mourning and weeping over oneself.

If we agree that an unconscious need for death-experiences is inherent in the drug addict and, less overtly, in our whole society, then we must apply this same archetypal perspective to the simple morning hangover—which can be a response to unconscious goals neglected when the cycle of drunkenness-hangover is viewed simply in terms of individual, pathological and compulsive behavior.

Going back to the categories we used earlier, we should ask if the individual is perhaps unconsciously seeking not only the regression entailed by an evening of drinking, but also the next morning's depression, and the process of its "working-through" and overcoming by means of a Kleinian reparation. We can see in the hangover a process of correction, both physical and psychological. The artificial excess of youthful vitality is transformed into heaviness, into a saturnine experience in which one's limbs seem leaden and one's thoughts gloomy, a sort of precocious senility. The middle-aged person who danced and joked like a kid the night before wakes up, the next day, full of aches and pains and dark gloomy visions with a life of their own. At first glance, the painful hangover seems a state of deathly emptiness, while drunkenness one of lively fullness. We justify many creative people's tendency to drink or take drugs in terms of their intense vitality—the artist is closer to the deepest roots of life, and drunkenness is an outlet for his almost constantly overflowing stream of libido, since this very libido searches out suprapersonal expressions and is not content with being confined to ordinary experiences. In truth, the artist is closer to the deepest roots of life and *of death*. For this reason he is drawn both to drunkenness and to the emptiness of the next day, which are, respectively, an archetypal summary and a metaphorical expression of life and death. Perhaps alcohol provided Hemingway not only with a strengthening of his already-unbridled vitality, but also, in the next day's flowing self-mutilation, a gradual experience of challenging death itself, a theme recurrent in his writings and in his life.

Drunkenness is often sought in a semi-conscious way, and the disenchantment and psychic mourning the next day is an equally important unconscious goal, especially for creative people. This is in fact the moment in which the individual feels himself most deflated from contingent factors and, if able to overcome the annoyance they cause, he actually feels the opposition of being and not-being more clearly than during drunkenness, an unstable and collective-bound state of mind. Perhaps it would be better to say that the opposition will now be a lived experience and not an abstract one; it will have been expressed and lived intensely during one single overnight shift of mood

Anyone researching the repressed aspects of our culture cannot help being struck by the fascinating paradox of waking up after drunkenness. In the midst of a world which evaluates according to criteria of rationality, this experience is irrational and intensely emotional. In a world which tends to produce and acquire more and more, this is an experience dominated by privation.

Our official culture seems to give little value to rebirth, not to mention repentance. But we shouldn't believe that something which has for so long belonged in the economy of the psyche can be eliminated without reappearing in unconscious and indirect forms. The spread of drug use is a product of our society and a warning about the weakest aspects of our culture. This is repeated over and over again in a commentaries on our present sociological situation. The continuing use of drugs represents, with its constant allusion to the need for death and initiation, a reprimand against our cultural one-sidedness. Not only the drug user but also the "normal" person, not only the sociologist but also the depth psychologist, is through the continuing use of drugs alerted to society's attempt at suppressing, in a utilitarian and rational way, the archaic need for rebirth.

CHAPTER 6

THE STORY OF "CARLO"

What attracted me most was the sensation of danger and of my own safety in those moments. The sensations I had were sensations of psychic completeness. . . . I think the case will be solved when I have those sensations in a normal state.

(Carlo)

Anamnesis and Drug Rites

I first met Carlo in the summer of 1975, when he turned up at the Zürich clinic where I was working. Despite his father's many business engagements, he had accompanied his son. Carlo's mother had neither a job nor household responsibilities, and even though she knew that she wouldn't see Carlo again for a long time, she had stayed behind in Italy.

Carlo had come to the clinic because he had a problem with drugs—a problem serious enough to warrant thinking that it could be faced only in a closed and protected place, by sacrificing the freedom of everyday life. He had been an addict for about three years. Since he sniffed *nitro* (a word he used to indicate certain paint thinners made with toluene and xylene), we can safely exclude the existence of any subculture tied to this kind of drug, especially in the Milanese hinterland where Carlo lived.

We know that when a drug starts to spread in a modern culture, the culture itself cannot officially accept it, but neither can it manage to eradicate it altogether. This is why, in practice, the dominant culture

71

allows for some subcultures as long as they do not become to trouble-some. Through its cult-of-substance, its own ethical code, rules and language, a group centered around a particular drug responds to the need for initiation repressed in everyday culture. The fact that initia-tion is rediscovered by these fringe groups does not necessarily point to the superior sensitivity of the groups themselves. The need to transcend one's situation is naturally greater for those on the fringe than for normal members of society.

Carlo, however, built up his rituals on his own and not in a group. Actually, use of the word "build" is innacurate, since it creates the impression that the ego is doing the work. In actuality, a whole subculture of rites and rules gradually emerged from Carlo's uncon-scious, and his ego was no more than a mediator, translating uncon-scious archetypal images into a communicable formula—words.

Carlo chose his drug in a completely unconscious way. He knew neither how nor why it acted upon his psyche, and he was completely unaware of the dangerous and irreversible organic damage it could lead to. Even though we are dealing with a modern industrial product, this substance plays the archetypal role of the exotic and sacred drug much better than the joints of marijuana so widely and profanely available to Carlo's generation.

Carlo's father worked like a dog to consolidate the results of his business success (he had a small factory in northern Italy, near Milan), and he did not admit—nor perhaps did he realize—that his marriage was not going well. If we wanted to tie his personal problem to a wider cultural one, we could say that he thought he had been nourished by an industrial, practical and optimistic culture. But behind this facade we can recognize a Mediterranean "Great Mother" with all of her melancholy and all of the invincibility of fate. Underlying the trust Carlo's father seemed to place in the ego, we can sense a person who feels buffeted by the forces of the unconscious. In Jungian terms, we can say that this man has a restless anima. The troubled or restless anima of his father—more than Carlo's mother—seemed to be the feminine element most influential in Carlo's life.

Carlo's mother, forty-one years old, had a difficult childhood from which she seems to have emerged a spoiled and indecisive woman with traits of irritability and hypochondria. Her husband's financial security allowed her to stay at home and have a household staff. But even the few commitments she had seemed beyond her strength. The situation became explosive when Carlo was born. Carlo—her first child—was sickly from birth and often kept her awake at night. She managed to put up with him for six months, then she took him to her mother's, in the southern Tyrol near the Austrian border.

This woman (Carlo's maternal grandmother) seems to have been the complete opposite of Carlo's mother. She was a kind of myth for the whole family, and her husband referred to her as "the saint." She was born into an aristocratic Austrian family, and had both strong faith and great patience. She was spoken of as a character from "the good old days" in the best sense of the expression. She was the most important person in Carlo's life; she is still his archetypal guide when he closes himself up in his world of fantasy. Her death was the single greatest blow Carlo ever suffered. Carlo's maternal grandfather was Italian; he was a cold, untrusting person described by others as somewhat crazy. He did not get along with his wife.

After what she had been through with Carlo, his mother had not wanted any more children for a good ten years. Then she had a little girl, about ten years old when I met Carlo. She gradually took after her mother as far as her hysterical behavior was concerned. A third child was born about three years later. Since Carlo's mother announced that she was absolutely unable to care for this child, he was almost completely entrusted to a nanny. Since the birth of this last child, Carlo's mother and father no longer had sexual relations, but one cannot help but think that even before that their relations were few and unsatisfying.

What emerges is a neurotic family structure which, as we said before, surrounds many addicts. Not only did the parents cease to have sexual relations, but they no longer seemed to have a relationship at all. One has the impression that the father dedicated all of his *eros* to his children, while the mother literally dedicated hers to her children's friends. By this time Carlo had friends who were grown up and his mother was still quite young and attractive; she would flirt and carry on with them.

Naturally this isn't something that I came to know of immediately or which Carlo's father expressed, since it seems that he knew nothing about it. This information gradually came out from the exchanges I had with Carlo, as he gradually began to have more trust in our analytic relationship.

Carlo displayed a great deal of bitterness as he told me about his mother's flirting. Not only was he hurt by her disloyalty towards his father, but he himself felt exploited. His mother, in fact, often went out with her son so as not to arouse suspicion, and then began flirting in his presence. When this happened, Carlo hated himself more than his mother, but his need for her was so great that he was willing to accept these subterfuges just to be able to feel that she also needed him, and to take advantage of the rare occasions he had to be with her. But this compromise became humiliating for him and, perhaps without being conscious of it himself, he began to feel deeply ashamed. But let us tell the story as it unfolded.

Carlo was twenty years old at the time, a tall, handsome and athletic young man. While he was in the clinic, his physique developed impressively. He dedicated many hours every day to body-building and worked especially on his chest, which gradually became bigger and more robust, though it was supported by two long, rather thin legs. We should recall Adler's theory of "organ inferiority"[1] in this case. Carlo's parents had always suffered from bronchitis, and he himself was born asthmatic. As a young boy he was also bronchitic, and the doctors prescribed mountain air. He gradually got over these complaints, but through unmistakable over-compensation. His chest and lungs apparently became the strongest and central elements of his adult physique. But they also seemed to play an important role in his psychic structure. As we shall see, Carlo allowed himself to be possessed by a seer/shaman archetype. The only drug that he sought in his self-initiation is one that could be inhaled. When Carlo went into a trance, his breathing became deep and noisy. The mutual conditioning between his altered breathing and trance state was so close that Carlo could often pass into his visionary state simply by using this particular type of breathing.

Obviously, not everything can be interpreted purely on a psychological plane. Certain organic phenomena are evident. It is only logical

---

1. Adler, A., *Studie über Minderwertigkeit von Organen*. Vienna: Urban & Schwarzenberg, 1907.

that the serious intoxication from nitro should have altered Carlo's breathing, just as it is logical that the intensified breathing should have brought about the trance in the absence of nitro, since an excess of oxygen causes changes in consciousness. But even if we could thus explain his total loss of consciousness, we would still not be able to explain the visionary/shamanic complex which took its place. Loss of consciousness results in the emergence of archetypal contents to fill the vacuum; but exactly what these contents will be is something that is determined by pre-existing and highly complex factors. One possible hypothesis might be that since both shamans and Carlo himself "fly" during ectasy, their relationship with the surrounding world tends to be concentrated on contact with air. When in a trance, Carlo in fact almost completely lost his sense of touch, while his sense of smell remained.

Let us take a look at how Carlo's particular psychology showed up during his childhood. As mentioned above, at the age of six months he was sent to stay with his maternal grandmother, partly to cure his bronchitis, partly because his mother could not take care of him. The mountain air of the Dolomites and his closeness to his beloved grandmother did wonders for Carlo. Within three years he was completely healthy. His psychological development seemed normal, though he became rather introverted. In his early childhood, Carlo had already experienced a radical regeneration, both in his interior life and in his relationship with his environment.

Carlo was subsequently returned to his parents in Milan. He had a hard time adjusting, even in speaking Italian (in the southern Tyrol, once an Austrian possession, German and not Italian is the common language). Instead of adapting, he became more withdrawn. He was about four years old by this time. Had he been seen by a child psychiatrist, he would no doubt have been diagnosed as partially autistic. It was during this period that Carlo was for the first time, in broad daylight, "possessed" by an archetypal psychic state like the one we normally experience only at night, in dreams.

Assuming a relaxed position, Carlo concentrates on one point of the brain. He realizes that he can speak with spirits (generally deceased people) and with the "thirteen senses" (at times these are his own extra-corporeal senses, and at others the personifications of these same senses). By passing over into this other dimension, Carlo is able to see his own future.

These experiences lasted about two months. Carlo realized that he was dealing with a world that was too powerful for him, filled with dangers, from which he knew he had to break away or risk going mad. He made an effort to break off contact with it. If we take Carlo at his word, these "conversations" seem to have impressively foretold certain details of his later life. It is equally impressive that he has so many memories of early childhood and that at such a tender age he was conscious enough to face up to and fight against the risk of psychic illness.

We should not forget the characteristics of the shamanic personality.[2] The would-be shaman is, from the beginning, a person who has tendencies towards trances and visions. When he is very young, he often has the feeling of having been called, of having a vocation, while at the same time suffering serious psychic disturbances. Naturally, a psychic disturbance itself doesn't make one into a shaman; what really counts is the ability to treat oneself and heal this disturbance on one's own.

In any case, it seems that Carlo was not meant to be a child like all the others. He tried hard to adapt and to be "normal" and to a certain extent he managed to carry it off, but the results (at school, for example) were generally below average. He improved every time he was sent back to his grandmother's. At the age of eleven Carlo was sent to a boarding school in southern Tyrol so that he could be near his grandmother; when she died shortly thereafter, he once again returned to Milan.

This time Carlo's marks at school were disastrous. He was always absent-minded and nothing seemed to interest him. He needed to be reborn, or simply to be born, since he didn't seem to have been "born enough." His actual material birth had been difficult, and he later grew up in an environment which only let him half live. He was confined to a limbo where all the various circumstances not only did

2. Eliade, M. *Rites and Symbols of Initiation*. New York: Harper & Row, 1958; and his *Shamanism*. Princeton: Princeton University Press, 1964, especially chapters I and II. Lévi-Strauss, C. *Structural Anthropology*. New York: Basic Books, 1963, Chapter IX.

not encourage but actually repressed the possibility of individual development.

At the age of eighteen, Carlo was painting his motorcycle in an unventilated cellar. The smell of the paint thinner aroused his curiosity. He inhaled it, and all of a sudden his old images appeared to him once again, clear and strong as they had been fourteen years earlier. (Carlo is convinced that our relationship with "other dimensions" changes every seven years. We of course know that the number seven is considered magical in almost all cultures and times. One can't help wondering how important it is that Carlo's great transformation came about when he was twenty-one).

This experience was Carlo's self-initiation into a drug and intoxication new and unknown to him. It also marked a break with his previous life. His personality partly died and was partly transformed. The importance of the first experience of intoxication has been described by De Mijolla and Shentoub,[3] who speak of the "initiatory encounter" and of the "mythical" experience which becomes the model for later experiences.

Carlo began going down into the cellar regularly to inhale nitro. His grades at school became even worse. Nobody in his family knew about the nitro. His father, who believed in the healing powers of hard work and will power, took Carlo out of school and put him to work in his factory, in the painting division. By the time his father realized his mistake, Carlo was as familiar with the various paint thinners as a gourmet is with vintage wines. (In a simple yet vehement manner, he once told me that it is silly to think that Swiss products are better than Italian ones, since the nitros produced by the paint companies in Milan and in the Piedmont are much stronger than those available in Zürich).

A good idea finally dawned on his father. He sent Carlo to a school for goldsmiths. Carlo seems to have always had a talent (more manual perhaps than spiritual) for drawing and small sculptures. In the clinic he devoted much of his energy to the workshop. But unfortunately it was already too late, and Carlo's ability to express himself creatively

3. De Mijolla, A., and Shentoub, S.A., *Pour une psychanalyse de l'alcoolisme.* Paris: Payot,1963. Chapter 15, 3; p. 325f

through images had become used, above all, to externalize his nitro-induced visions. This tendency to reproduce visions (especially those experienced with the help of a drug) is quite common among the tribes of the two Americas and among primitives in general. This reproduction makes the sacred status of the vision official, and often associates it with some phase of initiation.[4] But there are many analogies between initiation in general—shamanic initiation in particular—and Carlo's practices.

Carlo's apprenticeship lasted three years. During his trance states he was instructed by powerful voices as to where and when to inhale the nitro as well as the rites to follow when doing so. Very often the first presence that manifested itself was his grandmother, who acted as a kind of good guide. Carlo's apprenticeship was carried out through separate communication with the three elements which with he had been in confused contact with during his childhood:

—during the first year he spoke with the "future" (in a note he said that "the future has become my daily bread").

—during the second year he spoke with the "thirteen senses."

—during the third year he spoke with spirits and extraterrestrial beings.

The phases which the shaman must pass through are often divided into "three days" or "three years," etc.

In addition, Carlo also met "spirits of the wind" in his trances, and they carried him great distances. We know that shamans are very often attributed the ability to fly. Their visions are therefore not considered merely internal, but things that come from above, materially and through flight.

Carlo's relationships with women and his sexual life also reveal a certain analogy to shamanism. Both his relationships and his sexual life were unusual. He seemed to fall madly and naively in love with certain women, but he never had the courage to approach them. He had had sexual experiences, but they were for the most part disappointing, since he often found himself impotent (as with his

---

4. I have dealt with this question in a talk delivered at the IX Annual Congress of the Psychopathology of Expression. See Zoja, L. *L'Uso del depinto spontaneo e la Psicologia Analatica*, in Andreoli, V. (ed.), *The Pathology of Non-Verbal Communication* . Milan: Masson, 1982, pp. 89-96.

frequent disturbances of memory, this could be attributed to the organic damage caused by the nitro).

What interested him most, indeed the only thing that really seemed to interest him at all, was falling into a trance in order to have visions, and then to have supernatural powers at his disposal.

One thing should be said here in Carlo's favor. He never did anything in the hopes of obtaining material gifts. He would, however, be prepared to sell his very soul (as we will see from the third dream in the series we shall examine shortly) in order to have magical or extrasensory powers—what he generally called "psychic power."

Like a primitive medicine man, Carlo seemed to been called to this path, and he dedicated all of his energies to it at the expense of material things. If we reflect for a moment on what was discussed in the previous chapter—the model of consumerism being the antithesis of initiation, and how the former brings about the failure of the latter—then this lack of consumerism in Carlo becomes more understandable and confirms that he was potentially a true initiate.

Like a witch doctor, Carlo was interested in healing magic, but he did not reject "black magic" either. Carlo lived in a world more "primitive" than that of so-called "primitive peoples." He ended up producing an incoherent hodge-podge of psychoanalysis, parapsychology and ideas taken from the cheapest kind of comic books. Stimulated by the language commonly used in the clinic, he began quoting Freud and Jung, and even went as far as having conversations with them. These conversations, which took place in a trance, were less spontaneous than his other visions and perhaps less genuine. He also went through a period in which he was an explosive font of ideas regarding the cure of other patients in the clinic, but these too were incoherent and sporadic. He declared that "when he grew up" he wanted to be an analyst.

Carlo displayed the complex and intense psychism and sensitivity, part hysteric and part mediumistic, typical of the shaman. Unfortunately he was unable to find a culturally coherent expression for all of this. The fault did not necessarily lie in his culture, which was obviously different from and far more complex then a primitive culture, but rather in his own limitations. The way he transmitted his visionary experiences, as well as his psychological discourse, was not believable. And yet he made no efforts to adapt, for he was uncon-scious of this very obvious lack.

Carlo will be "cured" by giving up not only his drug, but also the complex expression of his unusual psychism. He will not integrate the dissociated elements of his life, but rather will let them fall by the wayside. He is not capable of being a shaman because he cannot really cure himself.

Carlo often created rituals and habits which he felt he had to obey. To inhale his nitro he often went to deserted places, to the top of a mountain or a hill or into woods (here we find yet another analogy with shamanic initiation). He would create a sacred space and recite propitiatory formulas which were not, however, always the same. Then he would soak a rag and hold it to his nose. During his rites Carlo felt neither hot nor cold (the shaman too learns to dominate temperature) and he once remained out in the snow for hours on end dressed only in very light clothes.

Vomiting was often a part of his ritual. The smell of nitro can on its own be nauseating, but it would seem that Carlo's vomiting had a more psychic origin, and was unconsciously stimulated by a profound need for purification (we know that the first phase of renewal is loss and renunciation). Intoxication can bring about vomiting, but not necessarily dreams of vomiting, which Carlo experienced a long time after the intoxication itself.

Dreams and Healing

We have briefly mentioned some of Carlo's dreams, and we will now look at them closely. Carlo had many dreams, but I have very few notes of them. Most of the notes I have were written by Carlo himself. Parts of his notes, however, are illegible, for his handwriting changed completely from day to day. He displayed some of the charac-teristics of automatic writing.

Due to the scarcity of the dreams at our disposal, and the nature of the dreams themselves, I feel that it is impossible to see in them a real development towards a more mature individuality, or develop-ment in the clinical sense. What is of interest, however, is the presence of archetypal elements. We shall therefore recount some of his dreams, not so much to plot out the process of his transformation as

to illustrate the interesting analogy between Carlo's "interior stories"
and certain cultural processes of which he certainly was not conscious.
We should stress that Carlo had never heard of primitive rituals
around the use of drugs. He was actually an incredibly uninformed
person who had never read a book in his entire life, a fact unambigu-
ously reflected in his schoolwork. He probably would not have been
able to clearly define the word "rite".

The following is one of his first dreams about flying:

> I am flying in a glider, perhaps with my father. It is a biplane, old
> but solidly built. The earth is very far down and I am seated
> precariously. After a long flight I finally land. I meet the builder,
> who gives me the construction plans of the plane.

Here we can already see Carlo's unconscious tendency to live
removed from the earth, with a definite taste for risks, if not for true
self-destructiveness. Perhaps he allowed himself to be carried away in
this dimension without having much control or room to maneuver—
otherwise why would the image be of a glider instead of a normal
airplane?

In keeping with what we have sensed from Carlo's biography, not
only did his father seem unsuited to the task of bringing the boy down
to earth, but he was actually his companion in his break from it. And
yet one can hope that his meeting with the builder expresses a certain
readiness on his part to integrate more responsible masculine figures.

Now let us look at one of his first dreams dealing with drugs:

> I find myself at the top of a high, steep, dangerous cliff. In front
> of me are four tins of nitro laid out in the shape of a cross around
> a fire. I see a newspaper and read the headline: "Youth Kills
> Himself With Paint Thinner". I angrily throw the tins into the sea.

Once again here we see dangerous heights and isolation from the
everyday world. We can also see the sacredness of the archaic ritual
(the cross and fire), as well as the tempting proximity of death.
The connection between death, sacred ritual and fire evokes some
unconscious form of sacrifice which, as a phenomenon, is as archaic
and archetypal as initiation itself.

A few days later Carlo had another dream which does not deal with
drugs yet which is interesting because it illustrates Carlo's tendency
to throw himself into archetypal experiences, even dangerous ones:

> I'm in an abandoned castle. There is a vampire; I don't want to believe it, but then I feel his presence. I manage to get away from him, and cross a room filled with coffins. One coffin contains a witch. There is a legend which says that if a pin is stuck into the coffin, the witch will come back to life. A man pushes between me and the coffin, thus saving me and all the others from the reawakening of the witch.

We can notice that Carlo's association underscores both his naiveté and his lack of realism. A castle is not at all prototypical of a "normal" building, nor does Carlo give the impression of being as solid and well defended as a castle. Generally speaking, the castle evokes something unusual, the flavor of a fairy tale, something not of the ordinary world, like the scenes in his two earlier dreams. We should also note that the danger entailed by the awakening witch is not raised responsibly, but out of childish curiosity.

We can sense that the builder of the glider, the newspaper headline and the man who blocks the awakening of the witch have some value in common. A Freudian interpretation would no doubt speak of the reality principle. These three elements could also have something to do with analysis, but above all with a function of defense (third dream), of organization (the first dream) and of adherence to external reality (the second dream) in Carlo. Unfortunately it seems to be activated only in extreme cases. We might say that it was through the active intervention of this function that Carlo, at the age of four, made that great effort to break with the hypnotic fascination of the archetypes. This same function will make it possible for him, with great effort, to pull away from the enchanted world of nitro.

In this sense, these dreams would seem to be "prophetic." They do not express a prophesy as such, but they show an internal predisposition towards positive development. The second and the third dreams show, however, that this function consists above all of censoring, not of a true evolution. From what I was able to observe, Carlo would later save himself from nitro by giving the impression that the unconscious richness he had expressed earlier was fading into an apparently banal bourgeois life.

This same sort of thing happens quite frequently among drug addicts with tendencies toward rich visions. It gives us the impression that if they manage to free themselves from the drug, then all their energy and strength will be absorbed in the monumental task of leading a normal life, where there is no longer any room for rich communication with the unconscious. I can't help wondering to what extent the analyst, especially the Jungian analyst, can genuinely help in such a process of liberation from drugs.

As we said earlier, physical intoxication is not, in itself, the problem facing the analyst. Communication with the unconscious, on the other hand, even if not yet a benefit in itself is in any case the principal means the analyst encourages and uses in confronting psychic illness. We thus cannot help expressing the doubt (without proposing an answer) that, in certain borderline situations and without being completely conscious of what they are doing, analysts might not be convinced that a total liberation from drugs really represents the greatest good for the patient. Even the medical doctor at times tries to limit drug use rather than eliminate it completely. But the doctor makes this decision out of pragmatism, since he feels that the end result cannot be reached. The analyst, on the other hand, might accept limited drug use for another reason—because he sees that a complete and total break with the drug is not desirable. By losing his accustomed communication with the unconscious, the patient might be left with too fragile a relationship with it.

The richness of the unconscious contents activated by drugs—their esthetic and almost mythic fascination—makes it hard to consider total abstinence as the greatest good. One could be led to seek not a total break with the drug but rather the "right dose" which would make it a friend. In the final analysis, the same sort of thing happens with medicinal drugs. To the Greeks, the term *pharmakon* indicated a substance both creative and poisonous. Time and greater expertise in judging the doses of various substances have allowed us to give greater importance to the medicinal value of inherently toxic drugs.

Once again we find ourselves face to face with an archetypal temptation, the archetype of the "magic herb" we discussed in the third chapter. Associated with it is the archetypal counterpoint of the sorcerer's apprentice, who obtains disastrous results even by using good powers, and the wise men and expert magicians who know how to use even evil powers to a good end. But the activation of this archetype leads us analysts to identify in some way with the wise magician. Even were we able to establish a safe dose, we would not have avoided the real danger—lack of awareness of the archetypal urge, which guides the patient in his various expectation about the drug.

But now let us return to Carlo's dreams. A great number of his dreams dealt with flying and contained very archetypal elements far removed from everyday life. Here is an example:

> I am communicating with a squadron of U.F.O.'s piloted by extraterrestrials. I meet one of them: a woman-robot made of plastic. I uncover her various anatomical part—she has no sexual organs. I then see the extraterrestrials land on their planet and I realize that life there is very similar to our own life. At the end of the dream I am riding a motorcycle the wrong way down a one-way street. I meet a traffic cop and realize that I have to turn back, getting off the motorcycle and pushing it along by hand.

A short time afterwards there was another dream which dealt with missing physical features:

> An organization of perverse outlaws, led by a Japanese, is mistreating some unwed mothers and blinding their children. I fight with the Japanese and save a girl whose child's eyes are without pupils.

In the fourth dream we see a relationship—both with a feminine figure and with sexuality—which is lacking, artificial (plastic), and distant (extraterrestrial). Is it really worth Carlo's while to run the risk of flying (a metaphor connected with the drug "trip" which separates him from earth) if this means having a more and more artificial and sexless relationship with women? And what if in the end it allows him to reach a world like our own? The evolution in the dreams—from the U.F.O.'s to the motorcycle, from the encounter with the feminine image to meeting the image of the superego—anticipates Carlo's re-entry into a more real and everyday world, at the expense, however, of fantasy. In the end, the real commitment is entrusted to the ego, to an act of the will, for Carlo will have to retrace his steps along the road he has already travelled without being able to use any devices (the mechanical means, the motorcycle) which he usually turns to when he wants to feel freer.

As far as the other dream is concerned, it could lead us to suspect that the conflict between good and evil is still too archaic, too archetypal to lead Carlo to a new consciousness. The potential element of development (the dream children, since they will continue to grow) is somewhat dubious in its origins (they are in fact all illegitimate). These children, however, have something which links them to the seer-shaman. Many cultures believe that the blind have, as a kind of compensation, "interior vision" which gives them wisdom and the ability to divine.

Carlo's gradual return towards reality is foreshadowed in another dream:

> I see a beautiful fertile valley. I see that one could plant some
> vines there.

Carlo, who now had to forgo his nitro, did drink a little from time to time. If we put aside for a moment the fact that alcohol can become as dangerous a drug as any, we can say that at least wine does not culturally and socially isolate Carlo like nitro does. Given that Carlo feels an archetypal need for ritual, we should point out that wine is linked to very widely accepted and "normal" rituals, while those linked to nitro are almost autistic. That Carlo's real need is not only for drugs, but for archetypal ritual linked up with the complete life cycle, is confirmed by the fact that Carlo does not dream of the actual substance, wine, but rather of the development of the vines. The implicitly recognized ritual concerns not only consumption of the substance, but the whole life cycle of the plant (we should not forget that one of the oldest written documents of Western culture, the lyric of Alceus, praises wine, gift of the gods, as well as the planting of the vines.[5] For the first time there is a positive element with maternal, natural and fruitful features (the fertile valley).

Here are two subsequent dreams:

> Another U.F.O. landing. Four characters get out but they were
> human beings. Anyone can change himself into a werewolf or
> destructive monster by drinking a certain liquid; in the dream it
> seems to me that it is nitro.

The seventh dream seems to remind us of the sacred importance of the extraterrestrials (there are four of them, a number associated with the cross) and to lead them towards the ordinary world; it suggests that even if one goes to other worlds, nothing really new is

---

5. See Diehl, *Anthologia Lyrica Graeca*. Leipzig 1936, p. 96; Lobel-Page, *Poetarum Lesbiorum Fragmenta*. Oxford,1955, pp. 346, 242.

discovered. In the dream, destructiveness and inhumanity are more closely linked to drugs.

My notes refer to many other dreams about flight, or attempts to procure a drug and carry out rituals with it. All told, Carlo's evolution was not great. We could say that his ambivalence about drugs was growing, and the negative characteristics of drugs more obvious. The drug never completely lost, however, its fascination and attraction.

Carlo's stay in the clinic lasted about a year and a half. There were some relapses during this period, but they became less frequent. It seemed to take a very great effort for Carlo to carry out his everyday duties (the rules of the clinic, the studies which he had to continue on his own, and so on). These great efforts left Carlo with less and less psychic energy available not only for carrying out his rituals, but even for becoming excited about them.

This life was "heavy" and Carlo no longer flew. The world of drugs had taken on more realistic characteristics, but that is not to say it had totally lost its fascination. Carlo confessed, for example, that his "conversations with the future" never really allowed him to know it in advance. But as the future arrived and became the present, he had the impression of already knowing it, a sensation of *déja vu.*. It was a reassuring feeling, and the reassurance itself was no less useful than the predictions themselves might have been.

Many readers will no doubt have read the report of Quesalid's shamanic initiation, reported by F. Boas and related by Lévi-Strauss in his *Structural Anthropology*. Quesalid seeks initiation not because he wants to start a new life, but because he wants to understand the tricks behind the medicine men's "miracles." He learns one of these tricks and uses it on a patient, but much to his surprise the patient actually gets better. In reality, it is not a miraculous power that acts to heal the patient, in Quesalid's case, or which raises self-confidence, in Carlo's case; it is rather the power of the archetype, of those most ancient, unconscious, impersonal and collective components of the psyche. This power is needed to accompany one through the phases of initiation and to encourage the development of the individual without isolating him from the surrounding world.

I didn't see Carlo again for six years. One day I was working with a patient when I heard a voice call me from the courtyard below. I went down to greet Carlo, who told me that he had been helping his father in the factory for some years. He was married, and no longer used nitro. He had a different, softer expression, though perhaps less interesting than before. He had also gained a little weight.

CHAPTER 7

FROM INITIATION TO CONSUMERISM

The World of Consumerism

Our goal at the beginning of this study was to find ideas and insights which might be of help in understanding the modern phenomenon of drug use, and this search has taken us in many directions. The time has now come to gather up the various threads and to draw some conclusions lest we find outselves with a handful of loose ends. Everyone would agree that the best way to look at drug use is to adopt an unprejudiced viewpoint. While not losing sight of the differences between various drugs, it is important that one should not consider any specific *drug* as "bad" or "good," but rather the individual's relationship with it.

This approach is supported both etymologically—there are no negative connotations to the names of specific drugs, but only to words referring to their unlimited consumption—and, above all, anthropologically. The least destructive use of drugs seems to take place in certain primitive societies, where it is part of a much wider and complex phenomenon. This has very little in common with the anxious and impatient use of drugs found in our society. "Primitive" drug use is preceded by acts of purification, by training and by sacrifice. It is circumscribed, accompanied and protected by rituals which continually guarantee its place within the larger context. If these conditions are respected, the use of a particular drug, rather than leading to regression, can contribute to the development of the personality.

The most degenerate and destructive aspects of drug use, on the other hand, are found in our society, where the humility and reverence for wise masters or for the paths set down by myth are all lacking. The type of drug use we witness takes place hurriedly, greedily and anxiously; despite a certain tendency among addicts to unite and form groups, the lack of common guides and common goals makes it a solitary business, equivalent to masturbation. The vision provided by drugs is not integrated into the surrounding culture, nor is there even a way of finding a place for it in the individual personality, and so it tends to fade as the purely chemical effects of the substance wear off. The drug then needs to be taken again and the risk arises of having to do so more and more frequently. The person who uses a drug cannot set the pace for his consumption. He might initially try to do so, but being alone, lacking rhythm, cadence, and outside support, before long his consumption is out of control and rolling along with the simple force of inertia. Like a tumor, consumption can reproduce and multiply slowly, steadily, and intractably.

With this perverse motivation behind consumption in mind, perhaps we can now take a second look at what was said earlier about the unlimited proliferation of drug use, and how this is due to the lack of rituals which could set a rhythm for it and contain it. The consumptive progression is inherent in our culture not only because of an absence of ritual rhythms as such, but because everything, especially our relationships with objects, is permeated by a pseudo-ritual, consumerism. This pseudo-ritual does not satisfy an individual's needs, but rather tends to continually multiply and increase them.

We therefore have to face up to the fact that in our society the initiatory model is no longer adequate for an understanding of drug use. We must integrate it with the model of consumerism, which was born where the sacred gives way to the profane, ritual to obsession, and the archetype to the stereotype.

We have already seen how the manic-depressive pattern, which is not only a clinical syndrome but also an archetypal model or a universal human potential, is increasingly split apart and unbalanced. For the very first time a civilization has, on one hand, tried to organically repress the experiences of death, mourning, and simple sadness. On the other hand, its goal—its ultimate goal, its hopes for the future, its substitute for all other transcendental goals—is not only the continuation of production and consumption, but their indefinite growth. Thus the archetypal polarities of the manic-depressive unity are split apart, and the second pole is denied in favor of the first.

The man in the street is no longer someone capable of both progressive bursts of enthusiasm and pauses for reflection, but rather someone who has made the manic choice, producing and consuming more than he needs. A hypothetical psychiatrist from some ancient culture (ancient Greece, for example, with its cult of moderation and self-control) who made the acquaintance of our modern-day everyman would undoubtedly find him decidedly dysthymic.

We are unaware of this unipolarity because we have lost our points of reference, and we all continue to live with the same expectation of continual progression. This expectation is shockingly unidirectional because it is so subtle, generic and unconscious—it is a prospective metastasis, or better yet, it *is* a metastasis, a psychological cancer. This limitless spreading of the vital urge, though denying death, can paradoxically bring it about.

The metastases of this cancer strike, in one way or another, our archetypal imagination. We can, if we want, disregard the findings of those researchers who have been studying the psychological elements in cancer; their conviction is that repressed elements can contribute to the development of the disease. But even if they were to be proved completely wrong, their error would still be meaningful in that it would correspond to a typical archetypal fantasy—that repressed psychic contents, when accumulated uncontrollably in the unconscious, help spark off a process of organic proliferation in the body, connected "sympathetically" with the repression. Even if this hypothesis could not identify an actual material process, it would still allow us to at least assert the existence of a psychological process which, according to the research, grows out of an archetypal fantasy on the theme of infinite progression. The argument is as important, in terms of symbolic or archetypal formations, as fairy tales, myths or the fantasies of psychotics. But isn't the archetypal fantasy of metastasis active to a certain extent in all of us? We tend to view cancer with fascinated horror. We believe that our horror is due to the deadly way the disease spreads. But over and above the quantitative side of the question, might not there be something in the very pattern of that spreading which hypnotizes us, which strikes us as being unavoidable fate, and thus an archetypal urge?

Why haven't we imposed the same taboo of silence on other diseases as serious as cancer, why haven't we euphemised them as well? "A terrible illness" we are apt to say, but are other diseases, a heart attack for example, pleasant? Other illnesses and diseases might strike us as serious, but rarely have they as magical and "unnatural" a nature as cancer. Here we see reproduction as a force serving death instead of life.

The problem of metastasis seems to be a serious one for modern man, both in medical and in psychological terms. The metastasis of need and consumption, and of the very rhythm of life, all reveal their more secret, unconsciously destructive forms in the person of the drug addict caught in a spiral of ever greater doses at ever shorter intervals. This might be why his drama awakens a sense of ambivalence in the public, along with that horrified fascination aroused by cancer itself.

The knowing and willful suicide of the drug addict—who breaks away from life not by renouncing it but by "consuming" in an ever more paroxysmal way—attracts our interest because this behavior is metaphoric of uncontrolled consumerism and the deadly end it can lead to.

We should turn our attention to the fact that not only the act of taking a drug but the rhythm with which it is taken has something compelling about it. At times one has the impression that the individual is obeying a commandment, or some transcendent power. We have not applied the term "ritual" to the drug addict merely by chance, nor would we apply it by chance to an obsessive person or even to someone who is simply tied to daily routine. We know that there are very close links between obsessive behavior and religious behavior; Freud even called the latter "the universal obsessive neurosis of mankind."[1] But if we approach the problem from the Jungian viewpoint, we know that religion and obsession are linked through their shared archetypal matrix. We would therefore not say that religion is causally generated by a compulsive mechanism, but rather that they are both born of the same underlying archetypal territory. Obsession can also be a need to "transcend" some precarious or limited situation; it becomes reduced to stereotypical behavior, however, and breaks off its search for meaning too early. From this point of view, then, the coercive character of obsessive compulsions is not only a simple neurotic mechanism; it also reveals the possibility of some underlying power.

The act of turning to drugs follows upon the need to transcend one's habitual state, and this unconsciously connects and unites the act with the religious urge or, to be more precise, with the aspirations of the mystic and his search for ecstasy. The establishment of a compulsive ritual, a barrier to transcendence, connects hypocritical confessional practices (it would be incorrect to call them "religious") with the gradual prevailing of regressive dependence on a fetish (the reassuring drug-object) in the search for ecstasy. The anxiety which many drug addicts suffer is often relieved not so much when their substance is actually taken as when it has been found and the individual knows that it is available.

The unconscious model underlying drug use thus has a religious tint, but in practice it is expressed, predominantly, through regression instead of progression. The most suitable mythical theme for expressing this pattern is that of Lost Paradise.[2] We have already seen, for example, that the real cleverness of the old man of Alamut consisted of a perverse exploitation, through drugs, of the need for paradise. The appearance of this regressive theme, a counterpoint to the pro-

1. Freud, Sigmund, *The Future of an Illusion*. New York: The Pelican Freud Library, vol. XII. p. 183.
2. For information on this topic, see Jacoby, Mario, *The Longing for Paradise*, Myron Gubitz, tr. Boston: Sigo Press, 1985.

gressive one of initiation, signals that the individual's relationship with drugs has deteriorated, and constitutes the psychological element connecting the initiatory and consumeristic models.

The search for Lost Paradise means that one wants to transcend one's present state for the sake of something sacred, not necessarily through a courageous renunciation of the ego, but rather through the restoration and the sacralization of a state of well-being. This sought-after state of well-being, already experienced in the carefreeness of early infancy, is sometimes achieved in fantasy. The underlying need is analogous to the underlying need of the consumeristic or obsessive syndrome.

As the initiatory model deteriorates into the consumeristic one, we not only witness the transition from the use which primitive societies made of drugs to the use which modern man makes of them, but also the descent from drug-initiation to drug-addiction. Among the various hallmarks of a relationship with drugs, that dominating at the moment of initial contact is above all the initiatory one. For someone who has never taken drugs before, the expectation of what will come from this experience and the initiatory expectation of coming into contact with another, higher, and more sacred dimension, unconsciously tend to coincide. This is true even if the individual, on the conscious level, is moved by more banal considerations, such as curiosity. As the experience is repeated again and again, and as the "profanity" of the user's earlier life becomes more and more accentuated, he is forced to suppress his archetypal expectation ever more deeply. Repetition supercedes initiation: religious expectation gives way to destructive obsession.

And yet even amidst the subsequent gradual self-destruction one can perceive the unconscious remnant of ancient sacred themes. Some deteriorated remnants of the ancient and universal propensity to sacrifice can be recognized in the drug addict's self-immolation. Sacrifice aims at sacredness (sacri-fice, "to make sacred") through the immolation of a victim; in more dramatic cases this victim was the celebrant himself. Couldn't we see the drug addict's slow suicide as a de-ritualized and unproductive sacrifice? This would lead us to suggest that there exists negative sacrifice, sacrifice where only the destructive part of the act survives, and which is carried out by that person we have termed a negative hero.

Sacrifice and Self-sacrifice

As we continue with our enquiry as to whether there are still active traces in our society of traditional models of passage, we need not limit ourselves to Eliade's analysis of the initiatory model; we can also follow the path of Mauss, who examines the sacrificial model. There are shared elements in the two approaches, even though one is interested in the religious function and the other in the social function. According to Hubert and Mauss, the basic outline of sacrifice is "the establishment of communication between the sacred world and the profane one by means of a victim, that is to say something which is destroyed during the ceremony."[3] What we note is that death (in important sacrifices, the thing which is destroyed is some form of life) is a necessary passage, a central experience, as is the case with initiation. In its most elevated form, as we have already mentioned, the victim and the celebrant coincide—the protagonist of the rite dies, as is the case with initiation. Sacrifice has, however, a tripartite scheme which does not allow us to take the analogy with initiation further. If in ordinary sacrifice there is celebrant-divinity-victim, then in cases of self-immolation there generally appears another element, the external beneficiary. In the case of Christianity, this is the whole people, all of mankind. Christ therefore brought this ancient religious procedure to its greatest extension, and also to its most radical simplification. (In this case, all three elements— sacrificer, victim and divinity—coincide). On one hand, Christianity elevates sacrifice to its greatest purity, making all of humanity a beneficiary, and upon the sacrifice founding a new vision of the world. On the other hand, however, Christianity makes sacrifice essential, it monopolizes it, makes it something sublime, something that cannot be repeated.

The new vision of the world that is ushered in is, both psychologically and politically, monotheistic and centralistic. Compared with this great Christian simplification, specific or differentiated sacrifice

3. Hubert, Henri, and Marcel Mauss, *Sacrifice: Its Nature and Function*, Halls, W.D., tr. Chicago: University of Chicago Press, 1964.

is no longer possible, because, as far as sacrifice is concerned, the final word has been spoken. After the self-sacrifice of God himself, who would even dare to sacrifice his dog or his donkey? The advent of Christianity ended up, in practice, suppressing the ritual of sacrifice and the psychological necessitites it expressed. The concept of initiation was similarly affected by the advent of Christianity. Initiation aims at the rebirth of man by conferring a new power upon him—the power of a mythical figure, and thus the power of the archetype. Initiation links man with myth, an immutable paradigm, thus granting him security and making him untouchable. Eliade points out that this is the reason why initiation is so central in traditional societies, while virtually absent in our profane Western society, where man is not confined to the re-actualization of myth, but is left on his own with the serious task of "making history."[4]

According to Eliade, it was above all Christianity that brought about this change, devaluing mythical models by entrusting man with the task of redemption. In addition, Christianity preaches a message of salvation to everyone, not just to initiates. With its openness to the masses, Christianity condemned the initiatory religious sentiment of the Greek-oriental mystery cults, dominant until that time, to gradual extinction.

We should add a few considerations to what Eliade has already said. No one could say that Christianity is lacking revelation, or a model to guide the individual, or that Christianity is uninterested in overcoming the natural man, or in bringing about the rebirth of the consecrated man through the death of the natural man. But this consecration is essential and absolute, open to and equal for everyone. There are no other paths; there are as many paths as there are men, and yet the path is really only one—the one opened up by God. Baptism takes the place of rites of passage. Likewise, there are no other truths to impart but the Word. The passage has been simplified as much as possible, and as a result initiation is open to everyone, and to no one. It is accomplished once and for all, not only ontogenetically, for the individual, but also phylogenetically, for the whole of mankind.

4. Eliade, Mircea, *The Myth of the Eternal Return*. Princeton: Princeton, University Press, 1971.

As is the case with sacrifice, this new conception so elevates the religious message that the ancient rituals, more limited and tied to less ethical and less absolute conceptions, were made insignificant or placed beyond man's reach. Initiation thus disappears as a differentiated, specific possibility, flexible and therefore adaptable to various needs. And so it disappears completely, because its transformation is not concerned with just an aspect of its ritual, but is rather part of the monotheistic development which gradually led to the modern world—a search for the One which, in structural if not ideological terms, establishes a relationship between Marxism and Freudianism on the one hand, and Judeo-Christian thought on the other. Nietzsche's re-evaluation of the Greek polytheistic spirit, Jung's archetypal approach and Hillman's corollary[5] all serve to counterbalance, on the psychological plane, this reduction to the One, a tendency which denies the complexity of constantly-resurging psychological realities in favor of the unitarian demands of the ego.

Initiation was therefore progressively denied by European culture, partly because it was perceived as belonging to simpler cultures, cultures that had been surpassed, and partly because it tended to be associated with esoterism and the formation of groups of initiates, while creating the conditions for the birth of subcultures and sociocultural groups which had overly autonomous and separate value systems. With a few brief exceptions, such as Gnosticism, esoterism lost its legitimacy with the rise of Christianity.

An authoritarian decree may eliminate initiation as a practice, but it cannot eliminate the fundamental archetypal demand, which ends up expressing itself in simplified surrogate forms and then deteriorates because it is unconscious. We have already seen that a typical example is the kind of group which offers solidarity and, with drug use as pretext, elaborates a code of behavior—a paradox, because the simple act of turning to drugs is less arbited by taboo than is initiation itself. Consumption does not clash with current values—indeed it was consumerism that opened the way, and the path of consumption is blocked only because of the toxic nature of the drug and the practical disadvantages it causes.

5. Hillman, James, and David Miller, "Psychology: Monotheistic or Polytheistic?" in *The New Polytheism*. Dallas: Spring, 1981.

Both the attempt to return to a form of initiation and the attempt to ritualize and institutionalize drug use (secretly, of course) appear to be not individual but collective reactions, cultural countercurrents which clash with the psychological monotheism of the ego and reason, and with the ideological monotheism of reduction to the One. Initiation seeks to reintroduce less reductive conditions and existential justifications, while the use of drugs, especially hallucinogens, offers the prospect of a polytheistic psychic economy freed from the primacy of the ego—something offered by dreams as well.

It is easy to see why these phenomena do not remain segregated in subcultures on the fringe of society or which bear the stigma of criminal behavior. They tend to appear in a wider context, since after all we are not dealing with isolated cases of individual flights from reality or from society, but with "cultural" recourses justified by the excessive one-sidedness of our world.

Substitute Religious Experience
Initiation is unmistakably ambivalent. On one hand it expects the individual to remain silent as far as newly revealed truths are concerned, while on the other it asks him to contribute to the strengthening of the group by recruiting new "adepts." The stronger one's identification with the group and the new truth, the greater will be the influence of the second aspect, the urge to proselytism. We can see examples of this in the field of analysis. We know that analysis, with its ritual, its "revelations," and its promise of rebirth, is one of the very few modern forms of initiation. But how often have we seen people, once the analysis is concluded, go out and invest great quantities of energy in persuading others, perhaps not in the least need of it, of the value of analytical theories or practices? An ambivalent proselytism can be seen very clearly in drug users. On one hand, few people would be so unaware as to overlook the tremendous responsibility involved in abetting the spread of drugs. And yet on the other, the need to propagandize often emerges unconsciously. The user often describes his experiences in terms more or less unconsciously designed to arouse curiosity or envy on the part of others. What he really communicates to the listener is not so much the pleasure of the psycho-physical alteration he has experienced as

the prospect of regeneration which led him to the drug in the first place.

Conscious and intentional proselytism is usually engaged in only by drug pushers. The drug addict who is not himself a pusher is careful when he speaks to or about others, and shows a certain amount of fear at the prospect of "initiating" someone into drug use. When he speaks about himself, however, he lets himself go and often refers glowingly to the drug's fascination, thus engaging in a form of contented proselytism. It would be too simplistic to simply call such a person a hypocrite. He is sincere, though somewhat dissociated. He condemns intoxication and addiction, but at the same time he would like to welcome others into the ranks of the initiated and strengthen this sect of those who possess an additional "truth." In other words, he would like to involve others in the archetypal element, the third element in our schema, while sparing them contact with the first two—something he himself was not able to do, and something which for the most part is possible only given a sacred dimension, and that he has lost.

Since we are more interested in preventing drug use than in repressing it, we generally tend to look upon every positive evaluation of drugs suspiciously, even if the evaluation is only partially positive. Such evaluations can easily turn into propaganda. If we want to approach the reality of drug use neither one-sidedly nor moralistically, it is essential that we note that positive evaluations of the power of conscious-altering substances have come from people generally considered "masters"—creative people looking for creative possibilities in drugs. In recent as well as in ancient times, poets have sung the praises of alcohol; one need only think of Baudelaire and Apollinaire, who dedicated volumes to it. We have already pointed out that one of the factors leading to the deterioration of drug use is the lack of modern-day masters capable of guiding and limiting it. In truth, there are always some influential people who do not take a negative stance towards drugs and alcohol, but they speak from the distance of irony or philosophical speculation. Their position is then distant and abstract, realized only in books or films and plays.

Brecht and Chaplin both seemed to say that alcohol helped in creating a good-hearted and easy-going attitude; they created characters who were harsh and untrusting when sober, but who became more human and generous once they had had a drink. This same kind of indirect propaganda also concerned substances with which we are less familiar. Aldous Huxley[6] describes his experiences with mescaline in terms often nothing less than ecstatic, and in various works, William James[7] mentions that alcohol, or the inhaling of nitrogen protoxides, aids in reaching mystical experiences. In short, they saw these substances as aids in realizing the expectations which the young Freud sought through cocaine.

In a certain sense, Freud, like modern-day drug users, materialized and simplified his own expectations of an important revelation, projecting them onto the drug. The fact that from Freud's research arose the most esoteric of modern professional groups, the "caste" of analysts (and not some pharmacological breakthrough) confirms the impression that experimentation with new drugs and the activation of initiatory hopes occur simultaneously.

The problems raised by proselytism underscore the tolerance-repression dilemma, along with the ethical questions posed by the spread of drug use. We know that conciousness-altering drugs, even though there are differences among them, can, all things considered, have devastating physical consequences on the user. The psychic consequences are no less devastating. Recourse to drugs appears to be a recourse to substitute religious experiences, which is unconscious as far as the common man is concerned, but which is conscious in the case of particularly lucid individuals such as William James. In a certain sense this is deleterious, because although a "religious" experience is achieved, that experience cannot be successful, that is, a direct archetypal experience. Psycho-physical alterations produce an internal storm of images and states of mind analogous to those produced by direct archetypal experience—one experiences a semblance of the "numinous."[8] As a result, every other kind of experience is considered meaningless and insignificant, and one goes back again to the drug.

6. Huxley, Aldous, *The Doors of Perception*. London: Grafton Press, 1977.

7. See James, William, *The Varieties of Religious Experience*, chapters XVI and XVII. New York: Collier Books, 1961.

8. This idea, taken up by Jung himself in a number of places, goes back to Rudolf Otto. See his *The Idea of the Holy*. London: Oxford University Press, 1910.

The gods speak to us through drugs, but only from within, and gradually our relationship with the world is deadened. The gods speak to us, but without the mediation of a rite or the kind of protection that comes from a shared group experience. We haven't gradually prepared to respond to the voice of the gods, nor to really even listen. Any theophany is unbearable unless it takes place in context of a faith. Every religion teaches that God is too powerful to be faced directly, for that would take us into the realm of what St. Paul terms the "terrible." If our participation in such an experience is not marked by a respectful and prudent distance, if we are without any sort of mediation, then we fall "into the hands of the living God," and his light and power can burn us.

CHAPTER 8

REBIRTH TODAY

Considerations on Types of Drugs

Thus far in our study we have treated the elements of depth psychology, the archetypal models, which accompany drug use. We have also assumed that no drug is inherently good or bad and that such categories should rather be applied to the attitude with which a person turns to the drug in question. And yet we are well aware that we have been talking about drugs through a sort of intellectual fiction. Our principal aim was not to refer to the actual substances but rather to the psychic themes which cluster around the idea of drugs and the archetypal expectations which we project onto them.

If we go beyond this intellectual artifice, we must recognize the fact that the term "drug" refers to substances quite different in their effects, and thus almost impossible to classify. Different people can have very different reactions to the same drug. A classic example is alcohol, which can make one person depressed and another euphoric.

Without entering a field we are not competent in, we can affirm that the use of drugs seems to exhibit two types of effects in terms of the structure of depth psychology. Individual substances can hypothetically be situated somewhere in between the two poles. Drugs help

103

facilitate symbolic experience by activating the products of the unconscious (the symbolizing effect); or they temporarily alter the relationship between the Ego and the Superego (the hypertrophying effect).

It is immediately obvious that hallucinogens are closer to the first
of these positions, while alcohol (and amphetamines, along with most
consciousness-altering substances) are closer to the second. This
division can help us on a distinction which we have already come
across, *i.e.,* that the sacred character of the substance which accompanies the various phases of initiation is most prevalent in hallucinogens.
Alcohol, even though it is drunk in groups and more or less ritually,
is never as much of a "religious agent" as hallucinogens because it
does not exhibit such a direct relationship with the symbolic and
imaginal experience. Alcohol influences the production of images
only at very high levels of intoxication, but even then the images are
generally limited. *Delirium tremens* is the most dramatic example.

Alcohol is used in certain collective rituals, not so much because
it fosters symbol-formation, but because it creates an atmosphere of
extraversion which in turn contributes to the cohesion of the group.
Gelpke (see Chapter Three) and others believe that societal tolerance
of drug use corresponds to that society's dominant psychological
attitude. Since extraversion is highly valued in our culture, alcohol is
more easily accepted in the West, while in the East, where the dominant culture emphasizes introversion, hashish is more widespread.

This distinction may explain why the use of hallucinogens seldom
causes either addiction or the manic-depressive circle one risks in
encounters with other drugs. With hallucinogens, the experience of
an altered psychic state has a marked symbolic character which does
not peter out when the vision, which is at its core, fades away. Many
feel that they cannot and indeed must not describe their visions,
which are analogous to those experienced during initiation. A slow
process of elaboration ensues, in which the individual ego continues
to carry on a dialogue with the symbol and allows itself to be influenced by the archetype behind the symbol. For example, after an LSD
"trip," even weeks later, one can still experience moments of internal
rapture during which one is inexplicably fascinated by an image or a
feeling. If there is a risk here, it is of psychotic degeneration—the

ego, especially if it has no external, environmental or ritual contain-
ment, can explode under the pressure of interior images, or of "the
living God."

Returning to the first of our formulations on the effects of drugs,
it should be pointed out that we spoke of the symbolizing *effect*, not
simply the production or perception of symbols. A highly symbolic
way of perceiving images is an important revelation provided by
drugs, but it is not the only one. The verb "to symbolize" means "to
throw together," to produce a new juxtaposition with startling effects.
On a "good trip," the drug user does not only perceive symbols, he
feels himself "symbolized," that a totality has been restored, that he
has been reconciled with an existential condition transcending the
here and now, and revealed an inexpressible meaning. He feels that
he has been restored, yet without losing his place in the world and
without losing his orientation in time and space.

Every symbolic experience is, in a certain sense, irreversible. It is
similar to that phase in the initiation process which leads to the
development of the whole individual. If, on the other hand, the
individual experiences hypertrophy of the ego instead of a symbolic
experience, then he will not cull any sort of productive psychic
richness from this experience; all he will be left with is the sensation
of having had, and lost, a certain power, or of having had a treasure
but lost the key. It is the restless desire to find that key that can lead
to further experiences with the substance in larger and larger doses
and at a faster rhythm.

If we define addiction or dependence as the acquisition of a habit,
all we have is a tautology. But we can also see addiction and dependence as a search—the search for a transcendent experience always
sought but never reached. One begins pursuing this goal more and
more frenetically, and soon a manic pattern has been established.

We traditionally look askance on new or foreign drugs and are
afraid of them, while alcohol arouses in us a good-natured indulgence.
Being "traditional" there is a certain wisdom in this attitude. Alcohol
is an inherently addictive drug and can create the most serious kind
of pathological dependence. What protects and contains the user is
not some property of the substance itself, but rather the ancient

ritualization of drinking. It is one of our age old customs, unlike the improvised rituals of, for example, Western opium users. In the venerable Italian *osterie*, taverns which epitomize ritualized social drinking, we get the impression, despite the amount of alcohol actually consumed, that there is a kind of instinctive sense of limit, and seldom does drinking lead to violence or inhuman behavior. But these *osterie* are filled with an older and older clientele, and the younger generation is not taking its place. The *osteria* itself is an old institution—from time to time one closes down and is not replaced. There is one just opposite my door. The owner is always saying that he wants to retire, and yet year after year he keeps on working. If he should close down some day, his customers would probably become solitary drinkers. These customers fill the *osteria* with song not only because the *osteria* furnishes an external occasion, but because it also activates the drinker's internal, archetypal conditions. Left on their own, these men would probably go on drinking just the same, but they would no longer sing nor would they get heated up as they do now in their discussion of politics, art, or sports. The only thing that would give any warmth would be the wine itself, whereas now the vitality and common enthusiasm of the *osteria* all contribute to the atmosphere. Again, although merely an impression, it does not seem that the younger generation has a specific and ritualized context for its drinking. In general, our youth seems to drink anywhere it can, at parties, in loud nightclubs, or simply on the street.

Perhaps some new ritual context might be created around drinking, but great responsibility is involved when a drug is transferred from one context to another. If alcohol were to lose its traditional Western framework, it would be well on its way to becoming a drug like all the others.

We do not know what sort of a pattern alcohol consumption will follow among the younger generation. We have, however, seen the sociological transformation of alcohol as far as female drinking is concerned. Its remarkable increase is closely connected to changes in male consumption. There was a time when men had a monopoly on various types of drinking, whether it was the drinking of wine with meals or the ritual drinking with friends in an *osteria*. In the past, because of cultural taboos and the absence of accepted rituals, women drank alone, and they drank above all highly alcoholic liqueurs. We have no traditional images or representations of a group of women drinkers. The image and condition of the woman drinker, traditionally lonely and embittered, prefigures the ritual degeneration of modern-day drug addiction.

There are still fewer women than men who drink alcohol and use other illegal drugs, but one cannot thus deduce that the nature of woman is less inclined towards drug addiction. Rather, there seem to be two cultural elements which keep women away from the use of alcohol and drugs. First of all, women have less free time than men; indeed the very concept of "free time" is a male invention. Secondly (and this directly concerns our thesis), the initiatory and esoteric model is and has been since ancient times predominantly or exclusively male. This means that women have had little or no access of their own to the more ritualized and less dangerous forms of drug use. In the degeneration and profanation of drug consumption, women, culturally speaking, seem to be the avant-garde. Men are still quantitatively ahead of women in terms of consumption, but this seems to be a gap destined to be reduced.

Distinctions between various types of drug users, for example on the basis of pre-established categories, and distinctions between various types of drugs may be important, yet in a certain sense they can be misleading. If our investigation is to remain depth-psychological and not socio-cultural or psycho-pharmacological, then our interest must really be directed towards the final, unconscious goals of drug use. For the most part, however, we are unaware of what these goals are, and so we stress the substance actually consumed. The near-sightedness of the conscious point of view is analogous to that degeneration, consumerism, from which drug use suffers when it becomes a goal in itself. This degeneration is today quite widespread, due to an atmosphere of passivity and lack of effort when it comes to transcending oneself and one's situation. The "meaning" of a given situation is whatever is immediately and superficially perceivable, a tendency which, in the field of mass media and communications, McLuhan has summarized with the phrase, "the medium is the message." This phrase was formulated to indicate the effects of the spread and abuse of "means of communication," but the formula also applies to the problem of consumerism and drug abuse. Drug use seems to be the instrument for setting up contact and for communicating with new psychic states; unfortunately, by taking these drugs, we gradually give up communicating with the beyond, and concentrate our attention on what was supposed to be the means to an end—the drug itself.

Through a careful analysis of the mass media, it has been shown that a violent television program, even if produced for didactic reasons, ends up spreading violence rather than inculcating the audience with an uplifting message. We likewise know that even though television may try to teach us something, what it teaches us in the final analysis is to watch more television. And so today drug use invites an individual to use the drug repeatedly and the symbolic experience ends up teaching the user nothing—for the simple reason that the experience is not carefully and respectfully elaborated, as it is in the peyote cult or in ritual drug use in general.

Thus far we have directed our attention to those models of psychic action known as the archetypes, which constitute an ever-present though hidden substratum. This approach is most fruitful, since it keeps us from isolating the individual from the collective dimension, and allows us to see the problem not only in terms of pathology, but also as an unconscious attempt to reach archetypal goals. It is these goals we are most instinctively interested in. They seem to be the real problem hidden under the ugly facade of drugs. Unless we manage to identifty the goal we are unconsciously striving towards, unless we understand our underlying need, then sooner or later it will demand satisfaction. If we are not conscious of this fact, then it will be difficult indeed to fight drugs and drug use. And even if we succeeded in defeating drugs themselves, the underlying need, which in our opinion is the need for initiation, would take on even more disastrous forms since it would not have been adequately satisfied. (We have already referred to the initiatory element in terrorist groups). For this reason the need must be understood, and only then can we answer it and allow it an outlet.

But an analyst is not allowed to ask questions about an outer reality without looking into the hidden motivations which led him to that investigation in the first place. We can't help suspect that studying the hidden archetypal structures (the need for initiation) rather than the visible framework (the world of drugs) is not only psychologically deeper but is also more gratifying, more exciting and more beautiful. The phenomenology—the visible aspect—of drugs in our society is anything but gratifying, exciting or beautiful. It is ugly, frustrating and discouraging.

We mentioned earlier that an analyst can seldom accompany a drug addict along the path of positive development. The drug addict is rarely even accepted as a patient. There is thus a risk that one might dive into the study of archetypal structures to avoid the less pleasant but more immediate aspects of the problem.

For the most part, the phenomenon of drug use appears in individuals who do not know how to accept life. Frustrations cannot be avoided nor can contrasts be resolved totally and unequivocally. We could say that the people who turn to drugs are those who, to use Malraux's famous expression, do not know how to accept the human condition. If the drug addict were to descend to this condition, he would have to realize that he has betrayed the original need for initiation by transforming it into a purely consumeristic need. But he doesn't face up to this; he reacts by escaping. He thinks that he can pay any price in order to be freed from the human condition. But the price is very high—it can involve economic bankruptcy, not to mention the ruin of his health, his emotional life, his spirit. Freedom from the human condition is achieved when one reaches moments of a "semi-divinity," but above all when an almost stable "infernal condition" sets in. One no doubt at some point starts seeking liberation from this "infernal condition." But since it is often impossible to revert to the human condition, all one can do is wait for the liberation that comes with death.

The study of the hidden aspects of drug addiction is then a welcome phenomenon, but at the same time we must make an effort not to become purely theoretical researchers. Should we fall into this error, we would commit the drug addict's own mistake: we would be denying the human condition, with its ugliness and its irreconcilable contrasts.

Obstacles to Initiation in Pluralistic Society

The fact that we are not suggesting ways to revitalize initiatory experiences does not mean that we feel such experiences are unattainable today. What it does mean is that our society is so structured that it does not provide any pre-established paths towards initiation. In the past, society itself provided a fixed and respected place for initiation in the community; therefore the *a priori* absence of initiation could be one of the unconscious reasons for the new widespread sensations of alienation and despair. Some researchers believe that this unconscious need has already found typical surrogate forms of expression. Hocart[1] mentions at least three:

1. When a practice once generally accepted but now abandoned is revived because of a specific need—for example, when parents who normally would have neglected to have their child baptized decide to do so because the newborn is sickly.

2. When people turn to another culture with its rites and resources because their faith in their own rites has run out—the case in many religious or ideological conversions.

3. When ancient practices are reinstated, not because their real initiatory aims are recognized, but because of other rationalizations. An example is the popularity of the practice of circumcision—justified for hygienic reasons—in the United States.

Hocart's reflections exemplify what we are talking about quite well, but they do not contain general hypotheses about the deterioration of the initiatory process and possible ways of restoring it. In a footnote to the first chapter of this study, we referred to a phrase of Eliade's worth citing in full: "Initiation puts an end to the 'natural man' and introduces the novice to culture."[2] We could say, on one hand, that initiation is superfluous today, since the transitition that leads one into culture is no longer a difficult one requiring ritualization. Modern man is immersed in culture virtually from the moment of his birth. He never encounters a purely natural existence. On the other hand, it should be pointed out that modern man often feels he has been thrown into a particular culture or society almost by chance, which does nothing to inspire a sacred

1. Hocart, A.M., "Initiation and Healing," in *Man*, XXXVII, 1937, pps. 20-22.
2. Cf. Chapter One, Footnote 5.

sense of respect in him; on the contrary, man's sense of nostalgia for his origins has grown so great that he often looks to the natural man as something sacred.

The need for initiation—to be reborn into a life endowed with new meaning—always exists, even if it suffers from ambivalence. The satisfaction of this need is more likely to be found in individual, solitary and unrepeatable situations than in the precarious groups we spoke about earlier. It is likely to be pursued by people with restless natures, and more out of an obscure vital instinct than out of faith in specific rituals.

Many initiatiory rites (for example, becoming a warrior) were specific to a given culture and disappeared with modernization. However, a certain ceremony survives in those elements dependent on nature and hence unalterable, such as birth, mating, or death. These and other basic facts of life which have always had initiatory overtones are still celebrated, but they have lost the indispensable characteristics of initiation. A person's first encounter with sexuality is a good example. Our modern mentality has understandably sought to overcome the moralism that once surrounded sex, but it has also done away with the taboos and the mystery connected with it. These taboos are certainly not reducible to moralism, but rather served to sacralize and safeguard the initiatory function of sexuality. The natural fact remains, but the real initiatory rite dies because at least three of its characteristics are missing: sacrality, irreversibility and absence of alternatives. Let us look more closely at these three elements, for they will help us clarify our analysis. We must realize, though, that our treatment of the question will not by any means be complete (for initiation has many elements) nor will it be exact or precise (for the various elements overlap; sacrality depends to a large extent on the irreversibility and absence of alternatives; irreversibility is, on the other hand, the absence of that alternative which is the simplest of all, *i.e.*, a return to the previous state, etc.).

As far as sacrality is concerned, the disappearance of the sacred and the disenchantment of modern society represent too big a problem to be dealt with here. We should however point out that in pre-modern societies the idea of what was sacred and what was initiatory often coincided, in the sense that profound contact with the sacred often was, *ipso facto*, initiatory. We are interested in various aspects of sacrality as qualities linked to the other two elements.

We can immediately see how the process of modernization has eliminated the irreversibility of the few surviving initiatory processes. Let us take an example. The crisis which religious vocations are going through is a serious one indeed. The number of priests continues to diminish as more and more requests for dispensation from vows are being made to ecclesiastical authorities, and these are being more readily granted. The causes of this vocational crisis are obviously numerous and complex, and a thorough examination of the problem would have to be made along historical and sociological lines. We might be tempted to think that the increased posibility of obtaining a dispensation could, psychologically, help convince an individual to enter the vocation, especially the individual reluctant to make a commitment as dramatic as that of the priesthood. But would this really be a "psychological" consideration? It certainly has little to do with depth psychology, for it confines itself to the psychology of consciousness. Since we believe that the psyche also has unconscious needs and archetypes, we could actually hypothesize the opposite, that the *reversibility* of the vocational choice deprives it of its radically transformative character, complete with the death of the old personality, necessary for the satisfaction of our need for deep psychic rebirth.

A similar consideration could be applied to marriage, which has long maintained its initiatory aspects (more in the Catholic tradition than in Protestantism, and more for women than for men). Legally sanctioned divorce is only a very recent phenomenon in many traditionally Catholic countries, a delay ascribable to the Catholic hierarchy's fear that we would end up with a veritable avalanche of broken marriages, and that since divorce dissolves the civil marriage but not the religious bond, people would turn to the former and ignore the latter. In point of fact there have not been all that many divorces. Compared with religious marriages, civil marriages have continued increasing at more or less the same rate as before. All sorts of hypotheses have been proposed to explain these facts, but since they do not concern depth psychology, we shall not deal with them here. As far as we are concerned, all we can do is take note of this reality and reflect on it together with another fact, that there has been an even greater increase in common-law unions than in civil marriages. These facts would seem to confirm the hypothesis that irreversibility is a necessary characteristic of the initiatory model. The institution of marriage serves a visible, legal function. But as far as its deeper effects are concerned, it also and above all has an initiatory role. If marriage loses its initiatory function by becoming too easily reversible, as civil marriage is today, then people are moved to act on their emotional ties more directly, avoiding an institution perceived as having only a bureaucratic and legal role.

Civil marriage just a generation ago was a rare and courageous ideological challenge, but now it is so widespread that not even an archconservative would waste his breath criticizing it. It has become an alternative to religious marriage that anyone can take advantage of. But, paradoxically enough, its general acceptance ends up favoring common-law unions. One thus renounces the visible institution, since when it can be substituted by conscious choice, like some consumer good, it loses its initiatory value. If one can choose, and if the choice tends to be more and more secular (i.e. less tied to taboos or respect for the sacred, more based on convenience), then the most reasonable choice is one that produces an immediate solution with neither formalities nor complications. What traditionally motivates man to face up to added institutional commitments is not so much the need for institutions and their material guarantees as the need for a ritual experience capable of satisfying the archetypal necessity of feeling projected into a new, sanctified phase of life.

Part of the nature of an experience of truth is the need to eliminate doubt and ambivalence. But if there exist many diverse external truths, then their contrast can be introjected and *activate* doubts. The only exceptions are those rare individuals who are extremely coherent as far as their own values are concerned, and who can simultaneously accept the natural presence of both external diversity (collective "truths") and internal diversity (when one questions oneself). The need for truth usually overflows into a simultaneous need for uniformity—what we might call the vertical need (because it reaches towards both the heights and the depths of our being) thus becomes a horizontal one as well.

The same is true for the experience of the sacred. By its very nature, it is all-embracing. But can I experience it as such if it encompasses, in a sort of metaphysical embrace, only the totality of my being? For most people this would bring about a sense of anxiety and loneliness. (Because of the stress put on this vertical solitary experience, the Protestant churches saw their congregations dwindling before the same thing began to affect Catholicism). The average man is used to the habitual nature of life in general, and he allows routine and uniformity to meter his existence. He cannot suddenly be made to face questions like the problem of truth, of responsibility and of free choice.

Economic and technological progress, together with the advancement of political rights, have given us a kind of freedom and space for choice that never existed before. The "cultural" response involves what Rathenau and Ortega called the "vertical barbarian invasion," and what Fromm called the "flight from freedom." This is the new role played by the average man, who *en masse* seeks to take advantage of this new space and freedom while refusing the responsibilities it entails. This new space and freedom loses its very sense if man loses his ability to choose.

Our liberal pluralistic society is tolerant, yet it is the enemy of the sacred. Unconsciously, most do not accept that the sacred can be sought in institutions which are different from their own, exist side by side with their own, and are apparently in conflict with their own—they simply abandon the sacred dimension for good, thus adding to their existing apathy yet another burden and another libidinal block.

The sacred is pre-rational and supra-rational; it must necessarily come first. It is therefore difficult to rediscover it in the various institutions between which one must freely and rationally choose. If a response to the hunger for initiation exploits freedom of belief by simply proposing new institutions, the results can be counterproductive. If religious marriage loses its initiatory meaning, it will not so much be replaced by civil marriage—more modern but even poorer as far as initiation is concerned—as by free common-law unions.

Traditional marriage, admittedly not very innovative, often arranged by one's family and often primarily concerned with producing children, was paradoxically richer in initiatory overtones than is marriage today. Technology and our modern customs (the use of birth control devices, the ease of abortion, the general tolerance of society) offer us the possibility of making choices and then renouncing them, and our various institutions (marriage, legitimate pregnancy) are thus denied their initiatory character.

It seems unfair to say that modern man has abandoned both rite and institution because he hedonistically refuses to give up any of his needs. It could very well be that modern man abandons traditional rites and institutions because the process of modernization has forced him to deny the fundamental need which they tended to satisfy—the need for the sacred and for initiation. One need only take note of how alternative rites and institutions immediately and stubbornly reappear.

We have gradually come to realize that the question of initiation is almost limitless. Some traces of it can be found in many of modern man's apparently rational behaviors. We must admit that at the outset of this investigation we never imagined that an analysis of the theme of initiation would lead us so far and in so many different directions. We must of course be careful not to even suggest that initiation is ubiquitous, for this would inflate the theme itself, and if we start seeing initiation everywhere, we end up robbing it of its value as a specific reality.

At the same time, however, the initiatory model affords us better psychological understanding of those phenomena where, compared with the socio-political outlook, the psychological viewpoint is inadequate. Archetypal models allow us to catch a glimpse of structures existing independently of historical configurations. Let us consider, as an example, the phenomenon of terrorism.

As far as its relationship with the law is concerned, terrorism is based on initiatory-esoteric norms which might in some way be connected with the distant world of drug addiction. Both terrorism and drug use have been the object of attacks on the part of official society, primarily through police action, but this with little success. Results are obtained, however, when connections are formed and collaborators recruited. Our drug laws are aimed at the pusher while tending to spare the user himself, or to make him into a collaborator of sorts. In Europe, after a decade of increasing terrorism, laws encouraging "repentance" on the part of terrorists has helped to block the strongest of these organizations in less than a few years. To the student of law, this demonstrates the advantages of juridical operations over military and police ones. This success was obviously obtained by the law, but in the eye of the psychologist, perhaps with the help of unconscious elements creating the archetypal predisposition necessary for this success.

The fact that certain terrorists have begun collaborating with the authorities has certainly led to the apprehension of others. But was the promise of a lighter sentence the only factor which led these terrorists to renounce their terrorist views? Certainly not, since even if they do obtain clemency from a judge, they still have to face the deadly threats of other militants who have kept their word. Most of the terrorists who "repented" justified what they were doing ideologically—they said that they wanted to come back into legal society because they had witnessed the failure of terrorism's "political plan." This explanation is no doubt valid in terms of the psychology of consciousness, and yet if we carefully try to read the unconscious elements in their declarations, we can't help wondering to what extent they were also influenced by the failure of a hidden esoteric and initiatory "plan." Were they more disillusioned by general rational considerations, or by the members of the secret group to which they had tied their destiny? In their declarations, these repentant terrorists generally attack not only the political positions of their ex-companions, but also their personalities and the lack of a spirit of solidarity in the group, just as we suspected and mentioned above.

But if one enters a group not with a complete and sacred act of submission, but through a secular and conscious, albeit trying choice, then it is possible to come out again, and the initiatory group is brought down to the level of a simple club. The very first "repentant terrorists" deprived the group of its esoteric component and therefore paved the way for internal collapse, while simultaneously the information they provided the police fostered external collapse. This is the real point. Aside from its lack of a sacred dimension, modern society is too complex and tolerant to admit any alternative group in which membership is irrevocable. Only with the greatest difficulty can structures be revived favoring real initiation, yet not degrading it into just another choice in context of the very consumerism one rejects as anti-sacral.

Can, for instance, ecological groups or new sects really be considered "alternatives" when after a year or two one can simply return to normal life? The very concept of "alternative" is in reality foreign to the theme of initiation, for "alternative" (from the Latin *alter*) implies a choice between two possibilities on the same plane, while initiation implies complete rebirth at a higher level.

This statement doesn't mean that considerations on the need for initiation should necessarily lead us to pessimism. Since our approach is based on archetypal categories, it presupposes that the nucleus of the psychic process remains intact, waiting for a more auspicious time to achieve harmony with the dominant culture, and is weakened neither by the lack of sacredness nor by the ephemeral existence of initiatory institutions in modern pluralistic society. Sooner or later, in one way or another, it will be able to exert pressure to restore or create institutions capable of providing it with an official and ritual framework for those truly interested, if not indeed for society as a whole.

Falling in Love and Initiation

Let us turn again to the institution of marriage and ask ourselves about its underlying archetypal nucleus. It is commonly believed that the roots of this institution lie in the natural act of falling in love with a person of the opposite sex. For the moment we have no intention of questioning this; all we should like to do is place the word "natural" in quotation marks and point out that we are interested in the close connection between falling in love and initiation.

To further clarify our position, we should like to turn to the distinction between falling-in-love and love proposed by Francesco Alberoni,[3] a student of movements and institutions. As a starting point, Alberoni uses the distinction between the *statu nascendi* and the institutional state. More precisely, falling-in-love can be seen as the

3. Alberoni, Francesco, *Movimento e instituzione*. Bologna: Il Mulino, 1977.

motivating force of a largely unconscious intention, while love is the
function of an informal institution made up of unwritten rules and a
pact between the partners.[4] What Alberoni has managed to do is to
categorize an archetypal dynamic.

The urge to transcend falling-in-love and move on to love corresponds to the urge towards initiation, towards elaborate rites and
formulas aimed at consecrating and containing the process of rebirth.
Falling-in-love and initiation are so fickle that they create both enthusiasm and anguish. They are eager to establish themselves as institutions, but unwilling to be reduced to such. Any holistic phenomenon
rejects such a reduction, as do both the processes of death-and-rebirth
and falling-in-love, which unconsciously recapitulate the initiatory
model.

The most controversial text on the theme of love is without a doubt
the one written by Denis de Rougemont.[5] His thesis is that love, as it
is expressed in our culture, as "passionate love," is a cultural peculiar-
ity of the West grown out of the evolution of Christianity, specifically
the heresy of the Cathars. Many people have critized the thesis as
being insufficiently documented, and others have criticized the author
for going too far. In any case, while Buddha and Confucius encouraged
man to attain a calm and serene distance, the figure of Christ associated
love with the themes we have already dealt with: renewal of a death-
rebirth process and the theme of sacrifice. In contrast to the founders
of Oriental religions, Christ proposes involvement without reserve—
with love and passion. Love is considered a painful, irreversible experience of transformation, as underscored by our culture's obsessive
equation of love and death, for instance in the legend of Tristram and
Isolde.

In love we can perceive a typically Western phenomenon: a return
of what has been repressed, an answer on the part of the unconscious
to our ubiquitous rationalism and positivism (not only does the urge
to fall in love not spring from the ego, but it actually opposes it). What
we are saying here is by no means new—it is similar to what we have
already said about other irrational phenomena, such as fascination
with death or negative heroism. What we perceive in passionate love

4. Alberoni, Francesco, *Innamoramento e amore*. Milan: Garzanti, 1979.
5. de Rougement, Denis, *Love and the Western World*. New York: Pantheon Books, 1956.

is the necessary consequence of what Christianity proposes (passion) and of the processes usurped by Christianity from primitive and pagan worlds and later repressed (namely, initiatory processes).

It is often said that when one speaks about love one is really referring to something undefined. If we want to continue with our line of reasoning, we find ourselves in the curious position of having to turn to the categories used not by scholars but by poets. Rilke, in a study on Mary Magdalen's love for Jesus,[6] says that his loss, thus the loss of one's love-object in general, is the indispensable condition for the full realization of a spiritual and passionate experience of love between two individuals. This line of reasoning reminds us of the link between love and death, which is, in the final analysis, a specific form of loss. Rilke's argument suggests that union with the object of one's love is not the final goal, since it is destined to be lost, but rather that it is an archetypal numinous instrument for arriving at a new condition endowed with new meaning. Love clearly has both a sacrificial character and an initiatory one. The act of falling in love does not so much bring about union with the beloved as renewal in the one who loves. The various lyrical poems on love affirm that in such a state one sees the whole world with new and different eyes, for one feels oneself a child again or, conversely, one has the sensation of being an adult for the first time. One's own consciousness is changed and reawakened.[7]   Falling-in-love thus appears to be an attempt at rebirth. We know that it tends to produce images, symbolic experiences and renewal, which Dante describes in his aptly-titled *Vita Nuova* (*New Life*). But there are some other less important details which nevertheless must not be overlooked. An obsessive symptomology often accompanies falling-in-love, the semi-conscious necessary repetition of certain acts or certain thoughts, in which we can see either a pathological element or a profound and frustrated need for ritual—the choice is ours. Falling-in-love is not only creative, but also anxiously obsessive, and this obsessiveness reveals its "religious"

6. Rilke, Rainier-Marie, "Die Lieber der Magdalena," in *Die drei Liebenden*. Frankfurt: Insel, 1979.

7. John Donne's poem "The Goodmorrow" beautifully expresses this idea:

I wonder by my troth, what thou and I
Did till we lov'd? were we not wean'd till then?
But suck'd on country pleasures, childishly?

need for rules, security, and for the safeguarding of the excessively fickle container that is the institution. Thus one suffers from a compulsive need to constantly recollect certain memories, or for instance to retrace one's steps along a certain street once walked by the lover and the beloved. A phrase or a name echo and re-echo in the mind like a kind of chant. Love is something so big and grand that it overflows unendingly; it is always looking for something that will help contain it, but this element is never found.

Without a doubt, love is so highly charged with energy that it can help counterbalance the one-sidedness of our culture. It can help meet and satisfy the need for initiation, or in more general terms, the need for the irrational, for the magical and for the emotional. But it has not been sufficiently institutionalized into cultural forms stable enough to satisfy that need.

Falling-in-love, like art, like the creative act of producing, is an unconscious phenomenon. But like art, it needs will power and strength of ego in order to be transformed from fantasy into a real event with a renewing function. It thus becomes irreversible (returning for a moment to the categories we used when speaking about initiatory renewal), and the object of love becomes truly sacred and irreplaceable. Like art, love is forced to be creative and original, because in the rationalism of the society which surrounds it there is no language ready and able to express it.

Virtually anyone can have a creative fantasy, but very few can make a work of art out of it. And likewise, virtually everyone can have the experience of falling-in-love, but far fewer move on to the stage of love, where fantasies of renewal are confronted with reality, and where one resists being overwhelmed despite the absence of pre-established rules. Little by little, one should stop living love as if "being carried away" by something outside of the ego, or as a transcendent unconscious urge. Love should be incorporated into the ego. But in general one passively experiences a state of ravishment, of alteration, until love finally passes—not unlike the drug user who lives new ecstatic experiences, but then waits for their effect to fade. For this reason, falling-in-love has from time immemorial been associated with fantasies of potions and magic charms. Drunkenness and falling-in-love have similar archetypal matrices, and they are both potentially initiatory.

An Individual Sense of Ritual

Radical renewal and improvement in the quality of life are still as possible today as they were in the past. It would seem, however, that today they are in many ways more gradual and less solemn. Our society is not made up of castes or impenetrable guilds, and marriage is no longer a lifelong and binding commitment. One therefore does not irrevocably enter a certain profession, take up residence in a specific place, or assume a specific societal role—one has simply made a choice which, at least in theory, can be infinitely re-formulated. But this secular mode of behavior compromises the initiatory potential that various "passages" could have. Amidst these democratic rules and categories, our ancient need for initiation does not abandon its expectations for adequate rites, but all it finds is the parody of ritual offered by obsessive repetition.

Let us consider the process of coming of age. In primitive tribes, the young person is sooner or later subjected to a solemn rite of passage which consecrates him as an adult. He is instructed in the rules which govern his new state. He therefore acquires all the knowledge that really counts. From that day on, this person's duties and rights are no longer the same as they were before. Though the participation of the will and of the ego are minimal, what is solicited is the participation (Lévy-Bruhl's *participation mystique*) of the unconscious elements of the psyche—the individual's faith (or credulousness), his sense of magic and of destiny, and his visionary gifts.

Now let us turn to a less primitive situation, the period of the waning of the Middle Ages. Young Marco Polo, thanks to the cultural and economic situation into which he was born, receives a good education, but his passage to adulthood is marked by a fantastic voyage. All of a sudden, Polo finds himself in a new, different and immense world. This leap into adulthood and into the unknown was destined to excite the imagination of people for centuries to come, and to serve as a sort of model for all those who wanted to transcend their old situation of life and confront the challenges of a completely new existence.

Today there are no more new lands to be explored. One learns and grows by studying rather than by exploring. At the age of eighteen, the law declares us adults, but the new eighteen-year-old feels no decisive change in his life. He knows that for five or ten more years he will continue to be economically dependent on his parents, either because he is not able to support himself or because he must complete his studies. He might know how to use a computer, indeed he may have grown up using one, but he knows that even if he should go on studying until the age of thirty or forty, he will never be able to learn everything that counts in the adult world. Total knowledge has disappeared. He might come close to something similar by delving into some very specialized field, but even this impression, like a mirage under the sun, vanishes once it is approached. Both emotions and knowledge have been emptied of the solemnity, associated with rituals of passage, necessary for the individual to feel that he is completely renewed and raised to a new level of life.

But we really cannot allow ourselves to fall into naive sentimentalism or pessimism. Those moments of instantaneous sudden change are long gone, as are those external solemn rituals of passage. But this does not mean that the passages themselves no longer exist. It would be silly to say that there are no adults who feel that they have really grown, that there are no elderly people who have the sensation that their total personality is different from when they were young. Modern daily life obviously has many repetitive aspects which eliminate one's sense of responsibility; these aspects certainly do not aid in the development of what was once known as the wisdom of the old. Relationships with objects in our modern world are characterized by a passivity and lack of creativity whose most noticeable feature is mass consumerism. All that we want (and our desires can be infinite) we can have, like a baby at its mother's breast. The passage to and through middle age and old age—when one returns, in the form of wisdom and memories, all that one received during life—is gradually disappearing.

And yet the framework and possibility of "passage" still exist, just as the possibilities of ritual still exist. No rite is as total as the obsessive one. For the obsessive person, rite is life, it is the only thing to which he will sacrifice his vitality. And yet his life is sterile, the most deadly type of existence possible. According to the myth, Sisyphus managed to negate death, and his punishment is to roll a stone along the same path forever. This punishment is significant, and it makes Sisyphus the patron saint of obsessives.

There is nothing more potentially ritual today than the hollow repetitiveness of daily life or the activities and thoughts which accompany an average day and permeate its every moment. Rites can no longer guarantee a sense of the sacred conferred from without, but can only guarantee that sacrality which is the fruit of an interior process, the gradual process of taking my experience of life and "making it really mine." Our experiences may be soulless, they may be repetitive impositions I must accept, but they can become "really mine" if I don't simply bear them, but choose them, if I move ahead as my own guide in life of my life. Both in the case of love and of obsession (which, as we know, is a corollary of love) we are faced with the task of transporting something initially perceived as external into the ego. Falling-in-love, like obsession itself, is a proposal which the unconscious makes to the ego; the former is the proposal of renewal, the latter, the proposal of order. It is not impossible to control a compulsive rhythm of life. Even though permeated with certain fixed tracks and repetitive elements, a normal day of city life allows for more choices and more conscious responsibility than that of the primitive, who could turn corners without looking at traffic signals, but whose ego was hemmed in by magical mystic forces. A day in our lives allows for freedom, though unfortunately we have not been taught how to use it. For the most part we don't bother to take advantage of this freedom, because what we do in life is not perceived as sacred or even meaningful. We are called upon so often to make choices that no one choice is followed long enough or coherently enough to transform our personality, or to be perceived as a vital goal. Within the repetitive rhythm of life, almost everything is relegated to external formulas and institutions which arouse enthusiasm for only a few moments before it fades away.

It seems to us that the possibility today of finding real collective institutions which can oversee initiatory passages is at best slight. But rites of passage still exist; they are gradual and last a whole lifetime. Our institutions neither recognize nor grant them importance; they are not to be found externally, nor are they ready-made. They arise from the rules which, over a period of time, we set for ourselves through self-discipline. The pre-fabricated life in which we find ourselves is almost soulless, and it therefore expects and demands a sense of soul from us.

The task before us is to cultivate the self-discipline (which is not the same as a set rigid of fixed rules) necessary if we want to gradually pass over from studying to knowledge, from falling-in-love to love, from ideological drunkenness to real political and social commitment, etc. If we develop this discipline for ourselves, then our "passage" is already consecrated. Of course, there is always a spontaneous urge to share this sacred moment with others. But the price of our secular and pluralistic society is the solitude and loneliness of such experiences. At most, they can be shared with one's beloved, with a fellow student, or with another person who shares the same ideological commitment.

There is nothing new in the idea that the old and progressively differentiated familiarity one has with a commitment one makes actually endows it with sacredness. The new viewpoint we are suggesting is that this process is equivalent to a modern initiatory passage. This is not simply a theoretical consideration, but rather something which I have come to understand from my analytic practice.

The work of analysis is simultaneously an affective process and one which clarifies and adds to consciousness. It is subject to rather rigid, but also ritualized bonds. It takes a long, gradual and difficult process of self-discipline for one to be able to assimilate what has been clarified by analysis in terms which are not solely rational. The same self-discipline is needed if the affective element is to be transformed from a form of projection into a genuine "love of self." If the process works as it should, it can be expressed as a sort of rebirth. This rebirth will be slow, tiring, expensive and incomplete, and yet it is one of the few experiences of rebirth which can be found with a certain degree of objectivity in our modern metropolitan culture.

As far as analysis is concerned, it and its setting are not pre-established sacred institutions, rigidly defined from the beginning. What is pre-existent and potentially sacred, however, is the need for rebirth that impels an individual to undergo analysis along with the obsessive necessity to ritually establish its various phases. An initiatory process can develop out of this nucleus, but not out of normative institutions or other external forms of authority.

INDEX

Other Titles from Sigo Press

The Unholy Bible *by June Singer*
$32.00 cloth, $15.95 paper

Emotional Child Abuse *by Joel Covitz*
$24.95 cloth, $13.95 paper

Dreams of a Woman *by Shelia Moon*
$27.50 cloth, $13.95 paper

Androgyny *by June Singer*
$24.95 cloth, $14.95 paper

The Dream-The Vision of the Night *by Max Zeller*
$21.95 cloth, $14.95 paper

Sandplay Studies *by Bradway et al.*
$27.50 cloth, $18.95 paper

Symbols Come Alive in the Sand *by Evelyn Dundas*
$14.95 paper

Inner World of Childhood *by Frances G. Wickes*
$27.50 cloth, $14.95 paper

Inner World of Man *by Frances G. Wickes*
$27.50 cloth, $14.95 paper

Inner World of Choice *by Frances G. Wickes*
$27.50 cloth, $14.95 paper

Available from SIGO PRESS, 25 New Chardon Street, #8748A, Boston, Massachusetts, 02114. tel. (508) 526-7064

In England: Element Books, Ltd., Longmead, Shaftesbury, Dorset, SP7 8PL. tel. (0747) 51339, Shaftesbury.